'This book is a real eye-opener for professionals involved in corporate and vocational learning, be it as policy makers, program designers, teachers, or trainers. In contrast to previous traditional approaches, the HILL model is strongly founded in recently advanced multidisciplinary research on learning and development. This innovative perspective on education opens multiple possibilities for designing more efficient methods that involve a major shift by placing the agency of learning and developmental activities in the hands of the learners themselves.'

– Emeritus Professor Dr Erik De Corte,
University of Leuven, Belgium

'*Creating Impact through Future Learning* is a very much needed book on effective high-quality learning in today's working life. It addresses the key question of how training programmes can help people to learn effectively in a constantly changing world. Even though the book has a strong scientific underpinning, it is very well written and motivates professionals to develop themselves. Furthermore, the book gives direction on how to create effective training programmes for both professional education and corporate training.'

– Sari Lindblom, Professor of Higher Education,
University of Helsinki

CREATING IMPACT THROUGH FUTURE LEARNING

Organisations today operate in a fascinating world where change is constant, fast and continues to accelerate. It is the combination of evolving developments such as technological advancements, globalisation and new ways of communicating through multimedia technologies that drive us to reorganise how we live, how we work, how we create value, and how we learn. These developments call for a Learning & Development policy and practice that supports professionals to be or become successful in this fascinating changing world. In other words: one of the core goals of Learning & Development is to support sustainable employability.

Creating Impact through Future Learning introduces a model for High Impact Learning that Lasts (HILL) that is very much in synch with the demands of an agile organisation. The HILL model is about the learning of young adults, professionals, and experts. It is about the many possibilities to inspire and to support adults in their continuous learning and development process, aiming to create value for today's and tomorrow's society. It is about how designers of learning programmes – be it L&D officers or teachers in vocational and higher education preparing adults for professional life – can take a step forward to build the future of learning. A new mindset is needed to create a real impact.

Filip Dochy is Professor of Corporate Learning & Development in organisations and education at the University of Leuven, Belgium. His research focuses on Learning & Development in organisational and professional education, learning and working in teams, virtual teams, competence-based learning, team–coaching, and the practical implementation of HILL.

Mien Segers is Professor of Corporate Learning at the Maastricht University School of Business and Economics, the Netherlands. Her research focuses on addressing workplace learning, aiming to provide insights on antecedents, determinants as well as effects in terms of employability and Innovative Work Behaviour.

CREATING IMPACT THROUGH FUTURE LEARNING

The High Impact Learning that Lasts (HILL) Model

Filip Dochy and Mien Segers

Routledge
Taylor & Francis Group

LONDON AND NEW YORK

First published 2018
by Routledge
2 Park Square, Milton Park, Abingdon, Oxon OX14 4RN

and by Routledge
711 Third Avenue, New York, NY 10017

Routledge is an imprint of the Taylor & Francis Group, an informa business

British Library Cataloguing-in-Publication Data
A catalogue record for this book is available from the British Library

Library of Congress Cataloging-in-Publication Data
Names: Dochy, F. J. R. C. (Filip J. R. C.), author. | Segers, Mien, author.
Title: Creating impact through future learning : the high impact learning that lasts (HILL) model / Filip Dochy and Mien Segers.
Description: Abingdon, Oxon ; New York, NY : Routledge, 2018. |
Includes bibliographical references and index. |
Identifiers: LCCN 2017050237 (print) | LCCN 2017054518 (ebook) |
ISBN 9781351265768 (eBook) | ISBN 9781138577879 (hardback : alk. paper) |
ISBN 9781138577886 (pbk. : alk. paper)
Subjects: LCSH: Organizational learning. | Employees–Training of.
Classification: LCC HD58.82 (ebook) |
LCC HD58.82 .D63 2018 (print) | DDC 658.3/124–dc23
LC record available at https://lccn.loc.gov/2017050237

ISBN: 9781138577879 (hbk)
ISBN: 9781138577886 (pbk)
ISBN: 9781351265768 (ebk)

Typeset in Bembo
by Out of House Publishing

Printed and bound by CPI Group (UK) Ltd, Croydon, CR0 4YY

CONTENTS

FIGURES

1

THE FUTURE OF LEARNING

Introduction

> 'Those who are crazy enough to think they can change the world, usually do.'
> – Steve Jobs

Organisations today operate in a fascinating world where change is constant and fast and this will even accelerate in the near future. Evolving knowledge in many domains, with technology probably as the most salient as well as being accessible worldwide, pushes organisations and in fact all of us to take the next step. With respect to technological advancements, over the next decade we can expect new smart machines to enter our lives in numbers we cannot imagine today, which will change every domain of our lives, such as teaching, health care, production etc. With regard to working life, one of the interesting consequences is that routine tasks will no longer be part of employees' jobs. Moreover, the availability of enormous quantities of data will change how we run a business, or manage work and our lives. We will be required to interact with data and make decisions based on patterns in data. Furthermore, our mode of communication is changing due to multimedia technologies. Moreover, demographic changes all over the world challenge us to rethink how to organise this next step. Given that in Western countries an ageing population is coming to the fore, we might expect that multiple careers will be commonplace, requiring us to engage in lifelong learning to be prepared for the occupational changes ahead. Moreover, for business, turning an ageing but well-experienced workforce into an advantage will require rethinking our traditional career paths and looking for more flexibility. Finally, globalisation is a trend that will continue in the near and far future with increasing exchanges and integration across cultural and geographic borders.

It is the combination of these developments that drive us to reorganise how we live, how we work and how we create value. In this context, for business, in order to create competitive advantage, the main challenge is to be (at least) one step ahead in dealing with the changes that appear on the horizon. Therefore, successful organisations position the topic of innovation high on their strategic agenda. Being oriented to innovation has multiple effects, not only on the work processes but also on the careers of professionals and their job content. Phenomena such as 'boundaryless careers', flexible jobs and job crafting are clear examples of this. Boundaryless careers result in the increased mobility of employees between employers and jobs. Fast changes in the labour market imply that we no longer work for a lifetime at a single organisation, such as our parents and grandparents did. Functional job flexibility leads to employees taking on different roles, tasks and functions as the organisation changes its strategies. Job crafting implies professionals that are designers of their own jobs. When I did my first job interview back in 1984, I received a phone call from the director the day after. He said: 'What do you want to know first: the good news or the bad news?' I insisted to get the bad news first. 'You don't have the job,' he said, 'we had another much more experienced candidate, with the specific expertise in the field,' he argued. That was a clear statement: I had no chance since I just graduated. 'The good news is that you can start next Monday,' he continued. 'We have some financial resources at hand, and you can create your own job at the skills laboratory,' he specified. Three days later, I started exploring what colleagues at the medical skills laboratory were doing daily. This idea was decades ahead of its time!

These phenomena have one thing in common: the search for sustainable employability. This means that in addition to professional expertise in terms of knowledge and skills as a basic condition, a great deal of flexibility to deal with change, and to anticipate it, is necessary for individual employees as well as for the organisation. In order to anticipate market dynamics, organisations use different ways to organise work than was the case a decade ago. A fascinating example is the rise of multidisciplinary teams as innovation incubators. By co-creating new ways of looking at and analysing the wicked problems we face in many domains of life, innovative thinking is boosted in these teams.

The developments that we have outlined and illustrated here call for a Learning and Development (L&D) policy and practice that supports professionals to be or become successful in this fascinating changing world. In other words: one of the core goals of L&D is to support sustainable employability. In this respect, there is a plea for organisations not only to invest time and resources in organising and optimising the quality of regular formal training programmes, but also to take advantage of the power of informal learning at the individual and team level by facilitating it. However, as Colin Powell stated: 'A dream doesn't become reality through magic; it takes sweat, determination and hard work.' So, where to start when building L&D that creates sustainable impact and how to make it happen?

High Impact Learning that Lasts (HILL)

For over 20 years now, scientists, Nobel Prize winners and practitioners have been warning that we are not learning effectively in our current training programmes.

Our upcoming generations of young (and older) adults could learn with greater impact. Moreover, the traditional teaching and learning methods such as plain lecturing have also been clearly proven to be largely ineffective. More up-to-date, active methods such as class discussion and collaborative problem-solving assignments have been shown to provide up to more than double the impact compared to passive methods of teaching and learning (Deslauriers, Schelew, & Wieman, 2011). What constitutes such an impact and why do we simply not increase the learning impact to that extent in all our organisations?

That is what this book is about, and that is what the High Impact Learning that Lasts (HILL®) model explains.

The HILL model is about the learning of young adults, professionals and experts. It is about the many possibilities to inspire and to support adults in their continuous L&D process, aiming to create value for the society of today and tomorrow. It is about how designers of learning programmes, be it L&D officers or teachers in vocational and higher education preparing adults for professional life, can take a step forward to build the future of learning. The developments described above make clear that there is an urgent need to rethink the future of learning. A new mindset is needed to arrive at a different approach where learners are in the driver's seat of their own L&D process and are supported in ways that create real impact.

This book makes abstraction of any kind of pursuing goals, qualifications and competences. The central question is: If we had to reduce a training programme to its essence or the key actions that create impact on learners and their learning, what would such a learning arrangement look like? It is thus time to take a step further: working and learning in teams, workplace learning, trust in partners, problem-solving, searching for information, selecting accurate and reliable information, being critical, creating engagement, entrepreneurship, and so on.

Recent developments in the learning society

Seeking knowledge is like opening many different doors.

New knowledge is being developed as never before. Mankind needed 14 years to double the amount of knowledge from 1930; in 1976 only six years were needed for the same and in the year 2000 knowledge could double in just one year. Nowadays, it seems almost scary to think about how quickly new knowledge evolves and grows exponentially. Universities and schools no longer have a monopoly in creating and transferring that knowledge. Certainly, in disseminating information and increasing its accessibility, the internet started playing an important role in the year 2000.

In the world of L&D, the fast-evolving and highly accessible knowledge should be a major asset. However, training programmes have for a remarkably long time stuck to the traditional learning paradigms. Content is well defined and ordered, lectures accurately programmed, and one can exactly control whether what has been learned can also be reproduced. And although such an approach is increasingly being heavily questioned, aspects such as active learning, learner agency, lifelong learning, openness, flexibility, problem-solving and other generic competences are still underdeveloped in many educational and training systems.

The traditional model of learning originated at a time when knowledge was inaccessible to most learners. Trainers and teachers acted within this model as gatekeepers that owned the keys to knowledge access. Today, many different learning tracks provide access to knowledge. Our gatekeepers see their function hollowing. Nevertheless, new questions arise, such as: How could the learner cope with this new stream of information? How to select a particular learning track? Which information is relevant? And reliable? Which criteria to use for that? How should all this information be structured?

L&D professionals and teachers have a crucial role in supporting the learner in effectively dealing with such a massive stream of information, finding a way in the jungle of information technology and, most importantly, transforming information into knowledge.

The labour market and generic competences

Do you realise that many jobs did not even exist ten years ago? Just to name a few examples: digital marketing specialist, social media manager, blogger, big data analyst. Moreover, many people no longer have a single 'job' that fits the kind of generic descriptions used before. Instead, given the dynamics in most organisations and the flexibility needed, professionals today fill a unique combination of roles and they switch and trade roles according to the needs of the organisation.

As a consequence, current HR practices move away from generic job descriptions. Instead, they stress the competences that current and future employees need to fulfil in their different roles, tasks and functions.

In almost every vacancy, organisations ask for employees with competences such as: flexibility, problem-solving, working in a team, creativity, critical thinking. This is in line with the many lists of generic competences that are published in different sources. We mention a few examples.

In 2001, the OECD published a list of core workplace competences that are most agreed upon by different analysts, surveys and country reports. In terms of interpersonal skills, this report lists teamwork and the ability to collaborate in pursuit of a common objective as well as leadership capabilities. With respect to intrapersonal skills, motivation and attitude, the ability to learn, problem-solving skills, and effective communication with colleagues and clients are mentioned. In addition, the report refers to the importance of analytical skills as well as technological or information and communication technology (ICT) skills.

In 2003, the National Centre for Vocational Education Research in Australia summarised the generic competences that most are commonly presented in listings. They ordered them into six categories: Basic/fundamental skills (such as literacy, using numbers, using technology); People-related skills (such as communication, interpersonal, teamwork, customer-service skills); Conceptual/thinking skills (such as collecting and organising information, problem-solving, planning and organising, learning-to-learn skills, thinking innovatively and creatively, systems thinking); Personal skills and attributes (such as being responsible, resourceful, flexible, able to manage own time, having self-esteem); Skills related to the business world (such as innovation skills, enterprise skills); and Skills related to the community (such as civic or citizenship knowledge and skills).

Looking to the future, the Institute for the Future of the University of Phoenix (Davis, Fidler, & Gorbis, 2011) published a list of ten competences needed for the 2020 workplace: sense-making, novel and adaptive thinking, social intelligence, transdisciplinarity, new media literacy, computational thinking, cognitive load management, cross-cultural competency, design mindset and virtual collaboration.

With respect to the workplace competences that have received most attention in research, Grosemans and Kyndt (2015) published the following list based on a systematic literature review: Theoretical business competences; Practical business competences; Problem-solving and analytical thinking; Learning to learn (in new domains); Time management; Managing self; Communication; Working in teams; Leadership competence; and Interpersonal competences.

Investigating what the labour market wanted in 2016, we came to the conclusion that priorities were given to the following competences:

• Working in teams	• Creativity
• Lifelong learning	• Knowledge creation and problem-solving
• Perseverance	• Information-seeking (accuracy)
• Critical thinking	• Engagement
• Entrepreneurship	• Self-responsibility

But how do you turn learners into problem-solvers if they cannot experience how to deal with problems and learn from these experiences? How to develop self-responsibility, meta-cognitive reflection and planning if learners do not have space to go their own way? How to learn to work in teams and to seek accurate information if the format is dominantly lecturing and individual rehearsal?

Although in 2017 many L&D programmes and professional learning tracks have moved away from traditional teaching methods, lecturing is still a dominant model in training, adult learning and higher education. Given the competences that the workplace is looking for, development/training programmes should offer real chances to practise communication and interpersonal competences, self-responsibility, acquiring new knowledge in a diversity of ways, self directedness, critical thinking, problem-solving, entrepreneurship, engagement, etc.

Even for initial professional training programmes, such competences are key since they train young adults for the professions of the future – think of big data doctors, AI creators, crowdfunding specialists, crypto currency bankers, privacy consultants, learning management system (LMS) designers, personal learning consultants, space workers, genetic counsellors, and the like.

Using information technology

Technology is the campfire around which we tell our stories.

– Laurie Anderson

The possibilities afforded by ICT have grown exponentially in recent years. Nevertheless, embedding ICT in learning programmes does not seem to be too easy. LMSs, electronic communication, and apps for cooperation have found their way into organisations that are stimulating a learning climate, but the role of these tools mostly remains rather restricted to electronic repositories of information and rather static ways to make information, assignments and knowledge available to learners. Research has not yet clearly demonstrated the advantages of ICT for learning purposes, other than an increase in the possibilities to bring variation into the learning process. Nevertheless, this phenomenon has led to a lot of applications of blended learning where variation is highly promoted, but very few of these applications are characterised by hybrid learning, i.e. a well-balanced mix between online and offline components.

Perhaps the high accessibility of video has been one of the most interesting developments in recent years. This had led to frequent use of webinars, flipped classrooms and integration of video in LMSs. Video can provide interesting possibilities to study cases at different locations, and an advantage of studying complex problems in this way is that the unravelling of the problem can be watched several times. The internet provides global information exchange and searches for information, and enables global discussions on specific topics.

In the upcoming years, a challenge will be to integrate ICT more effectively into our learning programmes. The same challenge accounts for the hundreds of different LMSs that are on the market. Communication and the active use of information is usually currently integrated in a rather static way: information is there to find whenever you might need it and the core of LMSs seems to be the delivered content (i.e. dozens of courses about broad hard and soft skills that are based on traditional courses or lectures). This surely supports blends, i.e. variety in the learning environments and methods, but it rarely supports a type of learning environment where learners are actively challenged and are learning deeply.

The crossroads where we are now

Our strongly enhanced access to knowledge, the exponential developments in information technology and the orientation of the labour market towards more generic competences, have brought us to the crossroads where we stand today. A crossroads where the road straight ahead is blocked, disappearing into a ravine. A 90° turn left or right is needed to head for new horizons. In other words, a re-orientation towards the core business of constantly updating knowledge, skills and attitudes (KSAs) is the way to go.

> *You are your greatest asset. Put your time, effort and money into training, grooming, and encouraging your greatest asset.*
>
> – Tom Hopkins

Employees are critical to an organisation's success. In the current dynamic world, they have to be up-to-date as well as continuously looking for new opportunities to further develop.

In order to fully engage in this ongoing learning journey, the learner has to be in the driver's seat. It is primarily his or her learning process. This leads to questions such as: How does the learning process proceed for each learner? How do they learn? What increases their motivation? What do they focus on when learning? These should be the guiding questions when redesigning any L&D activity. Starting from the learner's perspective, regularly checking to what extent you have designed an appropriate learning trajectory and to what extent learning activities are in tune with the interests, needs and possibilities of learners, helps to increase the impact of the L&D activity.

Continuous engagement and feelings of well-being are important indicators of success and of how strongly the challenges of L&D appeal to the learners.

How new is our current view on learning?

Based on earlier work and research (such as De Corte, 1995, 1996), about 20 years ago we framed different relevant characteristics of learning in powerful learning environments. New developments at that time (Poikela & Poikela, 1997; Segers & Dochy, 1999) gave rise to new views on learning and encouraged a different look at the future.

So, most components that are argued to be needed in future learning are not that new at all; some are even very old as can be illustrated by the 'learning by doing' principle (Dewey, 1938). Between 2000 and 2016, a comprehensive pile of evidence appeared in many journals, providing strong arguments for changes in views on learning from a lecture-based approach towards active, hybrid, science-based methods. These studies indicate that up-to-date learning activities have been shown to provide up to more than double the impact compared to more passive ways of teaching and learning (Deslauriers et al., 2011). As such, it is sometimes hard to understand why we still use words as 'teaching', 'lecturing', etc., instead of speaking about 'coaching learners' in their journey to expand their knowledge and skills.

Today, we are still working on implementing new characteristics of learning in our programmes. Relevant characteristics of future learning are seen to be the following:

Learning is an active process

Results of learning are directly dependent upon the activities of the learners. Learning is a verb, so trainers and teachers cannot take over. This statement has certain consequences. Making sense of the information retrieved, communicating, problem-solving, working in teams – just a few examples of the aforementioned skills – are activities that learners themselves have to perform. Learners need space to take responsibilities and agency.

Learning is cumulative

Learners relate new information to what they already know and interpret it by starting from their own prior knowledge framework. In this way, learners give meaning to new information. New knowledge builds upon existing knowledge, so the aim should be to strive for active knowledge building. Prior knowledge does influence the learning process: it can make a learning activity challenging for a specific learner or group of learners, while it can be irrelevant for another learner or group of learners. Learning assumes knowledge building on existing knowledge. Despite a lot of research on dozens of variables in learning, there are only two variables that strongly predict a large portion of performance: the learner's prior knowledge (Dochy, 1992) – largely intertwined with his or her interest and the learner's self-efficacy – his or her own conviction that he or she will just be able to do it (Van Dinther, Dochy, & Segers 2011).

Learning is a constructive process and learning is expansive

Learning is a constructive process

Insight in a specific area is not determined by the amount of knowledge one possesses but through the extent to which this knowledge is organised. What makes us an expert is the mastery of a flexible network of knowledge.

In other words: a well-organised knowledge base is created through actively threading new information into an existing base. Through flexible use in many diverse contexts (e.g. practice), one establishes new, more and stronger complex relationships between concepts and examples. Insight is mostly a process that comes during this flexible use. For example, for a small child with a newborn brother, the concept 'hospital' is just a place where children are born. After more confrontations with the concept 'hospital' in a diversity of situations, the concept will become richer and more complex.

Learning is expansive

A fast-changing society implies that we have to deal with questions and issues for which there are no answers yet. For L&D, it implies that people as well as organisations have to learn something that is not stable, often not defined yet or understood.

This means that we learn new knowledge and skills as they are being created. In this context, a 'competent teacher' has a different connotation than before. Teachers become facilitators and coaches, jointly dealing with the new issues to be addressed and developing their competences.

Learning is context-related

Knowledge is related to the specific activity, the context and the culture in which the knowledge is acquired. This implies that what we learn during training is not automatically ready to use in the workplace context. We might be able to solve the prescribed accounting problems during our accounting classes; however, that does not guarantee that we can successfully deal with our tasks when hired by an accountancy company. A starting point to help learners to make the newly acquired knowledge and skills ready for use in the new contexts they will encounter is to develop a variety of authentic learning tasks that challenge learners to engage in identical thinking processes to those found in the reality for which they prepare.

Learning is chaining constructive conflicts and challenge

The why and how questions are the most powerful levers for learning. Learning happens when there is an urgent need by the learner, when he experiences a gap in knowledge and skills, when he is challenged by a misunderstanding or a lack of understanding. Therefore, it is argued that learning is goal-oriented. Learners' self-defined learning goals largely determine what will be learned. For the development of L&D programmes, the challenge is to create flexibility in a way that programmes and courses stimulate the learner to go for the fulfilment of his/her own stated goals.

One way is to define problem tasks or assignments that learners can formulate (or recognise) as 'their problem'. Agency must surely increase if learners can (re)formulate the task themselves. This can encourage the learner to 'go for it' or to 'get it'. When learners are then confronted with searching for solutions that are not clear-cut (i.e. a cognitive conflict), they will experience a challenge that can lead to effective learning.

Learning is a matter of perseverance in working

In all fields of industry and in all areas of science, one can see many examples that show that expertise develops through deliberate practice. An excellent driver has a lot of experience and has practised in different cars, in different weather conditions, on different sorts of roads, etc. Famous inventors or innovative companies experiment a lot with many issues in order to achieve success with one issue (Edison invented the light bulb after hundreds of trials [and thus hours or days], but all his practice and experiments during almost 20 years at trying to extract metal from sand failed; Google is successful with Google Earth, Google Translate, etc. but did put lots of effort and hours in tools that failed such as Google Reader, Google Web Accelerator, Google Answers, Google Video Player, Google Buzz, etc.). An expert surgeon has practised for many years. Ericsson's research (Ericsson, 2016) shows we need about 10,000 hours of practice to reach expertise. Expertise arises through repeating problem-solving strategies in different situations and therefore gaining insight into which concepts and strategies are relevant to which specific situations.

A learning track should thus stimulate learners to use specific KSAs in a variety of situations in order to find out in what situation and under which conditions certain KSAs are useful. Offering a multitude of situations stimulates learner flexibility in using knowledge. Providing examples is not sufficient, since real learning appears when learners experience (and get the insight) that in a particular context other KSAs are relevant.

Knowledge arises and develops in teams and groups

The development of insights is enhanced through collaboration with peers and coaches. In this way, while learning cooperatively, learners can assess their own thinking and insights based on discussions with others. Collaboration enhances meta-cognitive processes such as reflection and in turn stimulates the deepening and refinement of insights. Learning in teams (Dochy, Gijbels, Raes, & Kyndt, 2014) and working in a 'learning community' (Savery & Duffy, 1995) are crucial as they provide the cornerstone for creating the social context for continuously being challenged by divergent ideas, for checking our own understanding with others, and in turn, updating our repertoire of knowledge and skills. Today, working in groups, teamwork or cooperative learning is not an option, it is a prerequisite for L&D programmes that aim for impact. This is not only because developing new insights asks for benchmarks – critical others to check the validity of our own thinking. It is also the case that the issues we have to tackle today mostly have no straightforward solutions and their complexity asks for a collaborative approach by a diverse group of people.

Learning is self-directed and pursuing your own goal

Learning is joy when the learner has a clear picture of what he wants, what he is after, and when he constantly traces (read: provides himself feedback) whether his activities have the desired effect. Engagement in learning increases when the learner is in charge and he has full responsibility for his learning. Learner agency is not possible without active participation by the learner. Continuous engagement needs to be fuelled by recognition, positive feedback and encouragement.

The way to High Impact Learning that Lasts (HILL)

The future we are facing is challenging in many ways. A fast-changing environment asks for fast-changing people. Therefore, continuous learning will be needed in order to master, fine-tune and develop competences that are needed in current workplaces and those of the future.

Recent insights into impactful learning are a relevant source to design L&D policies and programmes that are strongly in line with the demands of society in general and the workplace more specifically. The HILL model builds further on the scientific merits of recent decades and thus it should be no surprise that it implements core aspects of what has been discussed above.

The experience of urgency is the starting point of learning – prior knowledge is built upon through arousing interest; variation in learning experiences is the stepping stone to broaden and deepen your understanding; working in a team is the social context needed to answer complex questions as a learning experience in itself and to use cognitive conflicts as a lever for learning; learning is pursuing your own goals with a high amount of learner agency coached by others, expanding your KSAs with new knowledge and skills in the zone within reach, through hard work, sometimes in a state of flow (where time flies and hard work is fun).

2

AN EXECUTIVE SUMMARY OF THE HILL MODEL

High Impact Learning that Lasts

Starting from the challenges described in the previous chapter, we propose seven building blocks that can leverage the lasting impact of a learning situation. Together, these seven building blocks form a model of High Impact Learning that Lasts (HILL).

Do you remember a time when you learned something that you regard as your most optimal 'learning moment'? – when your learning experience was so strong that you will never forget the issue, you fully understand it and it will never ever disappear. Try to imagine that experience. You certainly still can see that moment before your eyes! Most probably with many details! Also the room, the location, the peers, the atmosphere, the joy, the excitement, the flow! Most of us can also remember these details. But if you now think about the real characteristics of that 'learning moment', what would you highlight as important characteristics? Many people then talk about, for example: we did it in a team; the experience was new; it was in real practice; we felt it was relevant; we did things, we were practising; we worked for a real company; we had chosen ourselves how to do it or how to learn it; the enthusiasm of people was affecting us; we needed the know-how for our own project etc.

All of these are the creators of real impact, and this is the core of this book. In this book, you will find an answer to the following key question: 'When and how do we learn in a way that has an impact; in a way that the learning "sticks"?' 'Impactful learning' is defined as engaging in learning activities that contribute to the development, fine-tuning, broadening and deepening of knowledge skills and attitudes and, in turn, supports the learner/employee to create or increase significant and unique value for his/her job and the organisation.

In other words, learning is considered as HILL when the learners enriches effectively his or her body of knowledge, skills and attitudes (KSAs) in such a way that the learner's professional functioning changes and consequently influences future situations in her/his working context.

The amount of research on learning, training, education, and development is extensive, and still growing. We started from our own research from the last 30 years, research on practices, training rooms and skills labs, and additionally overviewed all research on learning available in review journals such as the *Educational Research Review* and in electronic databases such as ERIC, Psychlit, Econlit, Medline, etc. Although some findings are contradictory and future research on several topics will be highly valuable to further improve our understanding of different mechanisms in diverse contexts, several main conclusions are clear and unambiguous. These main conclusions helped us to formulate a general answer to the key question addressed in this book that concerns HILL.

This book tells a different story, based on research and experience. It shows that the former paragraphs have almost no or a very limited impact while we nowadays know well what works and what creates impact. This involves not leaning back and listening, but rather being active, discussing and trying things out.

In addition to findings from research, trends in Learning and Development (L&D) practice have been published in many practitioners' journals and websites. For example, the 2016 CIPD employee outlook survey shows that employees are most likely to have received on-the-job training (28%), online learning (26%) and learning from peers (20%), creating a culture of ongoing knowledge sharing and collaborative working. However, despite the popularity of coaching, just 9% of employees said they had actually received it over the last 12 months. According to Lancaster (CIPD head), the benefits of employee-led learning in terms of team-work, knowledge sharing and longer-term employee satisfaction are significant. Learning should become an ongoing process in order to achieve long-term sustainable business growth. Highly attractive brand boxes for employees include the advantage of listening to newcomers (and old-timers) and understanding what and how they want to learn. Learners that do take responsibility, make their own choices and design their own development track, gain intrinsic motivation and take part in learning that brings considerable business benefits, according to Lancaster.

TABLE 2.1

Professional learning and corporate training are too often seen as:	Learning in programmes is too often seen as:
A forced choice from the catalogue	Attending lectures
A day off	A teacher explaining
Finding out what the expert has to say	Leaning back and listening
A pleasant day with colleagues	A final rush before the exams
A process involving relaxing and listening	Rapidly memorising and…
Seeing new developments and afterwards going back to the order of the day	Soon after again quickly forgetting

FIGURE 2.1 The HILL model

For newcomers, learning is key to unlocking their potential. Hiring a talent, if you find any in the future, is not enough. Continuous development is needed to achieve their full potential and a feeling of complete satisfaction for them. Frequent learning opportunities, such as provided by brand boxes at Google and Apple, update knowledge and skills and create sustainable workforces that are less interested in turnover and that are able to fulfil future competence needs.

Starting from a thorough analysis of the academic literature and resources for L&D practitioners, combined with our experiences with the practice of learning, training, education and development, we formulated seven basic building blocks for HILL (see Figure 2.1).

The HILL model is composed of seven building blocks that show no hierarchical relationship. In earlier attempts to create a hierarchy of building blocks, we consulted hundreds of experts and practitioners in learning and instruction, and always came to identical conclusions: all blocks are equally important.

The core of the HILL model

High Impact Learning is not a training or teaching method; it is a way to improve the impact of your learning programme. It provides a framework to analyse your way of working and to rethink your programme from a point of view of increasing the impact of your investments.

The seven building blocks serve as a guide for stimulating and facilitating impactful learning. In a nutshell, what are they about?

Urgency, a hiatus, a problem

Curiosity is the starting point, the key to learning. It is about being triggered by a phenomenon or an event that attracts your attention, gets your interest, although you do not (fully) understand it. It happens when a question is posed to you, highly relevant, highly interesting but no answer is available yet. It keeps you awake; you talk about it with your peers and friends; it triggers you frequently, etc. It pops up when you experience a problem that cannot be solved straightforwardly; it forms a hiatus you cannot fill easily, which challenges or even urges you to take action, to revisit what you already know and start from there a new learning journey.

Learner agency

HILL learning is about pursuing your own goals with a high amount of learner agency, coached by others, expanding your KSAs with new knowledge and skills in the zone within reach, through hard work and sometimes in a state of flow (where time flies and hard work is fun).

Time spent on learning is not a cost but a worthwhile investment when it serves you as a learner in dealing with the challenges you encounter and fulfilling the dreams you have. Moreover, you are in the best place to decide which learning opportunities to go for and when. It is most effective when you are in control. In short, learner agency is about acting as the entrepreneur of your own learning trajectory and requires you to be your own brand manager and portfolio manager.

Collaboration and coaching

Learning does not happen in isolation. It is much richer when it happens in interaction with others such as peers, clients, external stakeholders, managers etc. Those relevant others are not only sources of information. It is by sharing information, ideas, opinions and insights that misconceptions or gaps in your own thinking become visible. Other individuals fulfil the role of critical friend and coach. They stimulate your thinking, facilitate, mirror, appreciate; all important levers for growth and development.

Hybrid learning

Today, all learning is in some way blended e-learning. We blend teaching methods, media use, content domains, different modules, strategies, etc. But e-learning is mostly ineffective since dropout rates are generally very high. Only e-learning in a hybrid way can solve this problem. This is a well-thought-out mix between online and offline learning: face-to-face contact plays an important role in engaging the learning and fuelling the learning process.

Action and knowledge sharing

Experience is the teacher of all things, Julius Caesar said. During the past decades, many learning theories have elaborated on the importance of experience: you learn by doing, by undertaking actions, and this is even more powerful when it happens together with others, in teams, in networks, in communities. It is the dealing with and building upon the diversity in knowledge, experience, views and opinions in-action that turn an experience into a learning experience.

Flexibility: formal and informal learning

There is no one golden way to find an answer to all the questions that challenge you. As diverse as the triggers for undertaking a learning journey are the doors that can be opened to explore new insights, new skills, new ways of looking at a phenomenon. Asking a colleague face to face or in an online discussion forum, surfing on the internet, participating in an online course, participating in a conference or workshop are only a few examples of formal as well as informal ways in which learning takes place. Taking advantage of the flexibility in learning opportunities is an important stepping stone to broaden and deepen your understanding.

Assessment as Learning

Learning is a process in which you define your goals, make a plan of how to realise those goals, undertake purposeful actions and monitor progress by evaluating where you are in the trajectory towards the envisioned goals, reshaping where and when necessary. Explicitly monitoring progress through reflection and feedback is a fundamental part of the HILL model. Without this continuous process of assessment, learning cannot take place or will slowly but steadily fade away. Any assessment should be a learning event and not a stress moment.

A one-sentence explanation of learning in 2040

To introduce your manager to HILL, a quick overview of what the building blocks mean can be given by trying to express each block in one sentence. This will surely involve missing a lot of nuance and details, but it will provide a rough idea of what learning in the future should look like.

How to understand the model/What does it look like?

This model should be understand as offering a flexible way to enhance your impact. In our exercises with hundreds of people to settle a hierarchy of importance of the building blocks, we can only conclude that no layers or hierarchy are possible. All building blocks seem of equal importance and all can contribute to a higher impact of learning.

FIGURE 2.2 HILL blocks in one sentence

This flexibility means that you can start working on any building block. And in particular, we suggest selecting a few building blocks to work on and to optimise in your programme or approach. Step by step you can enhance your impact, depending on what your organisation and your teams find acceptable, supportable and realistic to implement on a pre-planned term.

 Do not implement all seven building blocks at the same time; A step-by-step strategy seems wise to follow.

In what ways is the HILL model relevant to you?

The HILL model is about the learning of young adults, professionals and experts. It is about the many possibilities to inspire and to support adults in their continuous

TABLE 2.2

High Impact Learning that Lasts:

Builds on what learners find urgent
Uses learner agency
Focuses on teams and appropriate coaching
Uses well-thought-out hybrid learning
Is based on action and takes knowledge sharing as key
Uses formal and informal learning in a flexible way
Promotes feedback, feedback-seeking, and Assessment as Learning

L&D process, aiming to create value for the society of today and tomorrow. It is about how designers of learning programmes, be it L&D officers, middle managers, or teachers in vocational and higher education preparing adults for professional life, can take a step forward to build the future of learning.

Ultimately, the HILL model can serve as a guide for everyone who has a responsibility for L&D. This in the first place implies the learner him- or herself. To build further on the words of Reid Hoffman,[1] be the CEO of your own L&D trajectory. Who else is going to be the CEO? If you abdicate that responsibility, then who will do it? The HILL model illustrates how you as a learner can shape your own L&D journey.

Several L&D programmes and L&D approaches in organisations have started to implement the HILL approach. We have seen outstanding applications: training programmes for sales reps where sales managers had to first go through the HILL model; learning programmes for business management where participants created their own track, their own project, supported by experts providing just-in-time 'flash-lectures' in the LMS.

Have you been inspired by the HILL model? You can read more about the building blocks of the HILL model in Chapters 3 and 4.

Note

1 www.businessinsider.com/success-secrets-of-reid-hoffman-be-the-ceo-of-your-own-career-2012-2?international=true&r=US&IR=T

3

SCIENTIFIC BACKGROUND OF HILL

As learning practice is constantly evolving and scientific research continues to investigate many subjects, we started our HILL expedition by performing three steps: first, conducting a comprehensive overview of theories of workplace learning that have been developed over the past decades (Dochy, Gijbels, Van den Bossche, & Segers, 2010); second, analysing the current state of the art in professional training programmes (Dochy & Nickmans, 2005); and third, exploring the changes that were seen in the last ten years of competence-based training programmes (Koenen, Dochy, & Berghmans, 2015). We also reviewed the literature from recent decades on learning, adult learning, professional training and development, transfer of learning, and workplace learning to look for consistent findings. Certainly, review studies provide interesting information. Just to mention a few examples: the pivotal review study on feedback by Kluger and DeNisi (1996) as well as the more recent review on feedback in teams by Gabelica, Van den Bossche, Segers, and Gijselaers (2012); the review study by Kyndt, Raes, Lismont, Timmers, Cascallar, and Dochy (2013) on cooperative learning; and the review on team learning by Decuyper, Dochy and Van den Bossche (2010). The results of this review of the literature are presented in this chapter. We aim to underpin the value of each building block, including three sections in the discussion of each building block. First, we start by briefly summarising what the building block is about. Second, we summarise how the building block is conceptualised and framed in academic theory and research. And third, we elaborate on the 'how to' question: how can we implement the building block into the learning process?

Building block 1: urgency, gap, problem

Small children learn because they want to explore their surrounding; engineers learn because they dream of building their own designed bridge or tower; sportspeople learn because they want to perform and win; I learned many things because I felt it would bring me joy and satisfaction.

What?

If you feel the urgency to know something, you will invest the energy required to learn it.

The 'sense of urgency' building block refers to the question 'Why do we learn?' So, getting learners to learn is all about triggers. It involves creating a situation where you are so strongly involved with what you do, what you are looking for, what you read, that you lose your sense of time. Your 'state of flow' erases the feeling that you have to make an effort. Can you remember when you last were learning something in such a flow?

I recently learned how to plaster walls. When I started reading a few articles online about how to prepare the walls and the plaster, and then started watching a dozen YouTube movies about different techniques, I really lost track of time. I worked for four hours and it felt like I had only been working for 20 minutes. Afterwards, I went off to practise on a wall and my sense of time again left me for half a day.

Such a sense of urgency can arise from a clear experience where a problem needs to be solved urgently (for example, a nurse who encounters once again a particular logistical problem), a strong argument (e.g. a written argument that a customer sends via e-mail) or the persuasiveness of the problem owner (such as a customer requesting consultancy). Or urgency can arise from a feeling of a strong interest in a phenomenon (for example, a learner or an employee who is interested in supply chain management or a natural phenomenon). So it clearly can arise from different sources: a client's request, a teacher's arguments, a discussion with friends, a simple experience, a story told by an expert, etc. These are the triggers that bring learners to a state of maximum involvement and intrinsic motivation for learning.

It is, however, clear that the feeling of urgency to learn cannot be imposed upon someone.

Why?

The importance of starting from the learners' need, or his/her feeling of urgency, to undertake learning activities is argued by many scholars. Within the traditional transfer of knowledge found in the training literature, it is generally accepted that a training needs analysis is the first step in a cyclical process of a training pro-gramme. It implies the identification of the learning needs of the target group. It should be noted that, supported by the results of a review study by Burke and Hutchins (2007), academic researchers urge for more empirical evidence to be provided on the specific role of needs analysis in realising transfer effects. However, within a different domain of research, more specifically motivational theories, there is ample empirical support for the notion of urgency as a powerful driver of learning. Probably one of the best known motivational theories, empirically tested in different settings, is self-determination theory with pivotal authors such as Ryan and Deci. In accordance with other motivational theories, self-determination theory positions intrinsic motivation as an important condition for impactful learning. The feeling of urgency is a strong intrinsic motivator. In the absence of urgency and without the motivation derived from the direct experience of urgency, learners may not be impelled to engage in learning. The challenge of engaging learners in online learning is a good example. Many companies nowadays have implemented online learning programmes. The problem many of them face is that, although the programme offers a variety of learning opportunities in a accessible way, the activity of the employees in the online learning programme is low. Only a small percentage of the employees participate in the online courses, access the variety of learning objects available (movies, reading material, assignments etc.), participate in the discussion forums, etc. This raises the question: How to engage employees in online learning? One of the strongest tools is making sure that the learner experiences the online learning resources as an easily accessible answer to her needs, the problems she faces and the challenges she experiences. Given time constraints, the employee is looking for the most cost-effective way to help her find an answer to a question or problem she is facing. If the online learning tool meets the employee's need for answers to problems on time and on demand, engagement in online learning activities increases.

Is every challenge a trigger for learning?

The answer is no. A challenge will only spark learning when there is an optimal balance between what the task demands from the learner (the challenge) and the competences of the learner (Csikszentmihalyi & Beattie, 1979). If dealing with the problem or the challenge is out of reach for the learner because it requires a level of proficiency that is much higher than their current level, there is no chance to become intrinsically motivated to learn.

Is experiencing a challenge, a hiatus or a problem sufficient to intrinsically engage in learning?

It is a necessary condition, because without motivation real impact does not occur and the learning process does not last. Learning certain issues just-in-time, or experiencing immediately the value of what you learn, or being able to use new insights in a project or in daily activities right away are key triggers that stimulate the learner. Starting from a perceived gap between what the learner can do and what she needs to do later, between what she knows and what she has to solve soon; starting from a specific problem or from a project that has a real problem owner, such as an organisation or a group, will cause engagement to rocket. It is precisely these aspects that can bring a learner to an additional energy investment in his or her own development and learning. However, more is needed to keep the learner in the flow of learning, to energise learning that lasts.

Self-determination theory stresses that for learners to be and stay intrinsically motivated, we need to create conditions supporting the individual's experience of competence, relatedness and autonomy. Competence refers to the need of human beings to understand how to attain the goals set and to be efficacious in undertaking the requisite actions to reach their goals and fulfil their dreams. The need for relatedness involves human beings striving for secure and satisfying connections with others in their social networks. The need for autonomy implies that human beings want to be in charge of their own actions, and, in the context of Learning and Development (L&D), of what, how and when to undertake learning activities. When we promote a learner's feelings of competence (for example, by giving positive feedback), support the learner in his need to be the CEO of his own learning trajectory (for example, by avoiding words such as 'should' and 'must') and help the learner to build a safe and inspiring network of learners (for example, by coaching teamwork), the learner will be more likely to retain his or her natural curiosity, to be intrinsically motivated for learning.

In addition, in the world of organisations as well as in research, a lot of discussions have been held about the power of rewards systems for motivating employees to participate in L&D programmes. Based on the results of the meta-analysis they conducted, Cerasoli, Nicklin and Ford (2014) advise HR practitioners to carefully consider which behaviour they aim to stimulate or reinforce through external incentives. A very strong incentive narrows down the cognitive focus of the employee. This is highly comparable to what too many summative tests do to college students. For example, suppose that in your company, for each new client contracted, the account manager receives a bonus of 10% immediately after signing the contract. This may be desirable in specific situations, such as the following: 1. where the task is clear-cut (for example, contracting as many clients as possible); 2. where the stakes for both the employee and the employer are high (for example, we are close to the end of the financial year and face a significant decrease in incomes); 3. where productivity is the most important concern of the management team; or 4. where compliance of the employee is crucial for performance or safety. However, directly salient incentives, such as tangible rewards that are promised by the employer and therefore expected by the employee, often disincentivise learning and intrinsic motivation for learning is crowded out. Furthermore, unethical or counterproductive behaviours may emerge. Negative effects of certain types of rewards might also play a role when we aim to mobilise learners in undertaking learning activities. This is especially the case when rewards are offered to people for engaging in a learning task without consideration of any standard of performance. For example, rewarding employees for spending time on the online learning program might stimulate them to log in, but not to really engage in performing the learning tasks. The same applies to rewarding general practitioners or other medical staff to participate in in-service training programmes by allowing them to increase the fee they charge to clients when they have been attending all of the meetings. It might stimulate them to show up at the meetings; however, it is far from certain if they will really engage in the learning opportunities offered.

Moreover, controlling incentives (such as measuring the time logged in on an online learning program) and reducing but **supporting incentives** (such as giving positive feedback on a discussion item posted by an employee in the discussion forum of an online learning program) enhance intrinsic motivation (Deci, Koestner, & Ryan, 1999).

In addition to rewards, are there other types of incentives to stimulate learners to engage in learning? The findings of the Cameron and Pierce (1994) review suggest that **verbal praise and positive feedback** enhance people's intrinsic motivation. The **quality of the learning task** also acts as a strong incentive in itself. Quality-type tasks, characterised by a challenging degree of complexity for the learner, require more significant personal investment from the learner than quantity-type learning tasks (where there is a high number of similar learning tasks). In the same vein, it is argued that **authenticity** – meaning that the learning tasks clearly match the real-life context in which the respective knowledge, skills and competences will be used – leads to greater intrinsic motivation. Authentic learning environments make it easier for the learner to identify with the learning material, to directly experience the relevance of it and therefore makes learning more meaningful.

'If there is no curiosity, there is no learning; if you are not a curious person, you are not a learner; if you are not curious, you are not a learner and therefore you won't learn,' said Dave Fox when I interviewed him on High Impact Learning. 'You create an environment where you strategise for learners to see how much reward there is in being a curious person' (Fox, 2016).

Building block 2: learner agency

What is your passion? What do you do in your free time? Horse riding or cycling? Or do you prefer to play chess, explore nature or enjoy paragliding? Assume that you were dreaming for ten years about horse riding and the day that you were due to start your first exploration, your father or your school teacher told you that horse riding was too expensive and too dangerous to learn, and they decided that you would be better off learning to play darts or play volleyball. Would you have been able to show the same engagement, enthusiasm and drive? And would you feel the same urge to make your next choice? Think for a moment about such comparable situations and the following question: If you can make your own choices, follow your own choices, create and conduct your own experiments, would you learn more effectively?

What?

> *The more people can decide for themselves, and the more choices one can make, the more they are truly motivated to learn.*

Despite the popularity of the concept of learner agency, how it is conceptualised and defined has been the subject of many debates among practitioners as well as scholars. Based on the definitions published by different scholars (Martin, 2004; Mercer, 2013; Van Lier, 2008), we define learner agency as the learner's awareness of responsibility for his or her own L&D, and accordingly the proactive engagement in learning activities.

Learner agency has become a popular term in discussions on professional learning, whether in schools or in companies, profit or non-profit. In educational settings, during the past two decades, student-centred learning has gained increased interest. Student-centred learning was a first modest step in the direction of learner agency, a first step in trying to take into account the learner himself. In the same vein, in the business world, employee-led learning entered the strategic reports of organisations. As the 2016 CIPD survey indicates, employee-led, or learner-led, integrated learning is the new normal. Learners choose their own development tracks as a major asset in the organisation's branding. Learning in the flow of work and initiated by work challenges has become increasingly commonplace. This has not occurred by coincidence. Organisations have begun to feel the consequences of demographic trends: too many seniors with not enough young people to replace them. So the new policy is clear: try to keep your seniors and keep them in development tracks; and at the same time, do the extraordinary to attract young potentials by offering them an attractive brand box. Hence, these young people see chances for L&D as a major asset.

Learner agency means that the decision-making authority and the agency over learning is delegated to the learner. As a consequence, learners are to a greater extent responsible for their own learning and there is a higher degree of autonomy in deciding how they act. Learners have to take this responsibility for their own L&D and to try to manage this learning process themselves to become more strongly engaged in the process. In some instances, the choices made by the learner can form his individual learning path. Learner agency also increases when the learner has a feeling of relevance. This means that the outcomes of the learning are clear and their importance is well understood.

Learners taking responsibility for their own L&D or learner agency involves self-regulation (Gao & Zhang, 2011). Being self-regulated first implies being aware of your own strengths and weaknesses. Next, the learner needs to engage in self-management. This includes setting your own goals and making decisions on how to reach them. Also, monitoring and regulating ongoing behaviour through planning is important. Finally, this also includes correcting mistakes by using the appropriate strategies for the different learning goals (taking into account the different constraints and affordances).

Here's an example of how I experienced learner agency as an ambitious but novice gardener. A couple of years ago, inspired by my father's passion for gardening, I decided to start my own little vegetable garden. Although while playing in the garden I had observed my father as he seeded and harvested for many years, in the process of planning where to locate the vegetable garden, I knew I still had a lot to learn. So, I searched on the internet, bought and downloaded books, and visited friends who had experience with biological gardening. It became a long and not always easy process where I had to learn from my mistakes, year after year.

For each decision, from the location of the garden to seeding and harvesting, I had to take into account so many factors: humidity, sun, quality of the soil, etc. I also had to make choices in terms of my goals. Do I go for a biological garden, a biodynamic garden or do I just want to be an ecologically responsible gardener? Do I want to tend a garden for fun, or do I want to be self-sufficient in providing vegetables for my family? The first year was not a real success: my salad crops were the favourite meal of a family of snails; the seeds of my green beans seemed to be delicious for the wild pigeons; and the broccoli plants did not grow or flourish. There were times when I was frustrated because, despite the effort, the harvest was so small. After my first year, my motivation to be a gardener was dramatically decreased. However, giving up was not on my agenda. Year after year, monitoring carefully what worked in my garden and adapting my techniques to the weather and soil conditions as well as taking into account my limited amount of time, I succeeded in harvesting a quite impressive variety of vegetables.

This example illustrates the core characteristics of a self-regulated learner. A self-regulated learner is intrinsically motivated and goal oriented. He or she monitors, regulates and controls his/her own learning during the different phases of task execution (from planning to action to evaluation), cognitively but also motivationally and emotionally.

Why?

Learner agency results in learning gains and improved performance.

There are many reasons why learner agency has become an urgent need for both individuals and organisations. The ideal of the working professional as entrepreneurial, self-responsible, flexible, creative, and as an active lifelong learner is inadequate if it does not consider the worker's personhood and subjectivity. A worker's commitment to the ideal of being a creative lifelong learner, someone who actively develops work practices with colleagues, needs large and active agency. This should be learned during professional learning programmes.

Professional agency (as defined by Eteläpelto,Vähäsantanen, Hökkä, & Paloniemi, 2013) is performed when professionals exert influence, make choices, and take stances in ways that affect their work and/or their professional identities. Agency is always exercised for certain purposes and is closely related to professionals' work-related identities comprising their professional and ethical commitments, ideals, motivations, interests and goals. Such a professional agency is needed to develop your work and your work communities (e.g. unit, team, department, network), for taking creative initiative, for professional learning and for building work-related identities in work practices. In recent years, various changes in the workplace as well as in education have escalated the demands placed on employees and students to take responsibility for and self-regulate their own learning (Sitzmann & Ely, 2011). A few examples follow:

First: in the workplace, the tasks to be performed and challenges to deal with are becoming progressively more complex and knowledge-centric, requiring employees to continuously update their knowledge and skills. Waiting for the next course to be available is no longer an adequate strategy. The more appropriate strategy today is to look yourself (as an employee) for suitable and on-time resources to deal with the challenges encountered.

Furthermore, in current L&D practices as well as in a growing number of educational programmes, learners are given control over which training courses they participate in and over the content, sequence and study pace of the learning resources. Next, in addition to formal training programmes, informal learning activities such as gaining new insights through discussions with colleagues while collaboratively working on a project, through participating in discussion forums or by checking media such as YouTube, are becoming more prevalent. These informal learning activities require the learner to evaluate and define what she needs to know (goal setting), and how and where to get it. In sum, learning as an employee and as a student is no longer a passive but a proactive, self-responsible process.

Not only within the focus of L&D, but also from a general organisational perspective, employee agency has gained a lot of attention in recent years. Studies reveal that employee agency manifests itself as self-actualisation, action and influence, which have implications for employees' psychological contracts. Employees emerge more and more often as active parties to the psychological contract, consciously modifying and constructing this contract, including their views on L&D.

Learner agency, exercised as self-regulated learning, has become more prevalent in the daily practice of the workplace and educational settings. In scientific research, the domain of learner agency and self-regulation in learning has received a considerable amount of attention, with pivotal authors such as Zimmerman, Pintrich and Boekaerts. The previous section on urgency referred to self-determination theory and explained that human beings have a basic need for autonomy, belongingness, and competence. By creating opportunities for learners to be responsible for their own L&D trajectory, we take the innate need of autonomy into account. When learners are empowered to make their own decisions when learning, they feel intrinsically motivated. It allows learners to fully embrace their own targets, to feel ownership over what they are doing and to see the time investments they make as a result of their own choices. It links the learning activities they perform with their own interests and curiosity.

Moreover, many studies consistently show that learner agency exercised as self-regulated learning significantly results in learning gains and improved performance. In their 2011 review study, Sitzmann and Ely conclude that current empirical evidence points out that trainees who engage in self-regulatory learning activities learn more than those who do not take responsibility for their learning process.

Individual coaching

Increasing learner agency is surely interconnected with methods of personal coaching. How do we coach individuals in such a way that their agency grows? Lazonder and Harmsen (2016) showed in their review of 72 studies that support has facilitative overall effects on learning activities, performance success and learning outcomes. Adequate support is not necessarily highly specific support. Findings show that less specific support leads to learning activities and outcomes that are comparable to those resulting from more specific guidance. Providing a context where learners have enough freedom to examine a topic and to perform a task on their own is certainly engaging. This does not mean support is irrelevant however: the type of support matters. Sierens et al. (2009) showed that autonomy-supportive coaching leads to significantly better results than controlling learners. This means that effective individual coaching provides freedom, time and a context to explore and to trigger the learner's engagement.

Coaches have a few elementary roles: ask the right questions at the right moments in order to help the coachee to tackle the problems he encounters. Coaches focus on the issues that the coachee raises; they praise, encourage, and provide positive feedback. Also, they do not interfere with the decisions that coachees take nor their consequences. In terms of L&D, this could be rephrased as focusing on continuous feedback and reflection. Certainly for adult learners, this is a very feasible but also a challenging way to progress.

A self-regulated learner – to be or not to be?

Sure, there are differences between learners in the extent to which they take responsibility for their own learning (Pintrich, 1999). Self-efficacy, interest and goal orientation predict to a significant extent whether learners engage in self-regulated learning. Research has been consistent in evidencing the importance of self-efficacy: learners who believe they can successfully learn and are confident that they have the competence to be successful are more likely to engage in self-regulated learning behaviour (Van Dinther et al., 2011). In addition, learners who are really interested in the knowledge, skill or competence that they are learning, who strongly believe that mastering this knowledge, skill or competence is important and useful, are more likely to engage in self-regulated learning. Moreover, the goals that someone aims to achieve influence the investment in self-regulation. When it is mainly about receiving a reward or promotion, increase in salary or good grades, learners may be able to attain this goal without much self-regulation. It might be more worthwile to do what you are told to do. You surely remember the exam you took at school, knowing beforehand already you would forget most of it soon after the exam. You simply did what was expected. For learning to last, to transfer to new situations, to be able to apply it in your daily job, a shift towards intrinsic motivation is required, where agency plays a real role.

 The three methods of training rated most useful by employees are:

(a) training from peers – 95%;
(b) coaching – 92%; and
(c) on-the-job learning – 91%.

(2016 CIPD employee outlook survey)

However, **only 9% of employees said they had actually received such training within the last 12 months**.

It is not only individual characteristics that account for differences in the extent to which learners engage in self-regulated learning. **Context matters!** If we are forced to learn something (e.g. at a specific moment) by a third party, and as learners we are inhibited from taking initiative, we create a cycle of dependence that prevents learners from taking a proactive approach, making choices, working at their own pace, etc. We risk ending up in a 'waiting room' modus, where we only execute a minimal effort to achieve what we are ordered to do. Does that ring a bell? Have you seen that happening? I have seen that many times; too many times. I have been a personal victim of falling into the waiting room trap too.

So providing choices is elementary for learning, as is providing a meaningful rationale of how this will add value to you as a learner. As I read Friedman's book on workplaces from my own 'learning' perspective, my attention was drawn to one of his quotes that I see as being perfectly applicable to learning:

Spoon-feeding instructions comes with a cost. Sure, overseeing every detail might speed up productivity on this particular assignment, but that short-term lift is likely to undermine your team's overall experience of autonomy, leading to long-term declines in their motivation.

(Friedman, 2016, p. 288)

It is clear that many programmes, regular training programmes as well as online learning programmes, offer ample opportunities to give learners the freedom to choose not only the content of learning, but also when, how and with whom.

Environment? Which environment?

In addition to offering choice, what are other relevant characteristics of an environment that not only stimulates someone to be a self-regulated learner but also supports the development of self-regulated learning (Boekaerts & Corno, 2005; Paris & Paris, 2001)?

First, offering tasks with a level of complexity that challenges the learners stimulates them to search for an answer or a solution, to try to really understand what is going on, to put effort and persist even when the first step is not successful: in sum, to self-regulate their learning, cognitively, motivationally and emotionally. These tasks focus the learners' attention on the task rather than the reward and sustain curiosity in the long run, keeping motivation going. This is the reason why teams dealing with complex tasks or problems are experienced as powerful learning opportunities by the team members. The complexity urges them to go beyond routine, to leave their comfort zone, to go into knowledge sharing and building with team members. A team of engineers, blue-collar workers and group dynamics specialists that have to develop a new app for increasing the safety of workers on the workfloor will have to think beyond daily routine, brainstorm about possible events and build together the know-how that will dictate the functionalities of such a tool.

Second, learner agency increases when the learners have a feeling of relevance. This means that the outcomes of the learning are clear and their importance is well understood. If a learner knows why it is important to reach certain goals, it keeps him motivated to learn and invest in his development towards these goals. When learners have their own goals clearly in mind, this mechanism works automatically.

I remember the many discussions with my children when they avoided doing their homework. The recurring 'why' question illustrated well the lack of relevance they experienced. The homework discussions mostly ended in rushing to finish the task just before bedtime, combined with a lot of frustration for both the children as well as the parents. A totally different situation appeared when project work was introduced in the programme and the children could define their own project. During a birthday party with their favourite french fries, the children started to discuss the origin of the word 'french fries'. They turned this into a small project which aimed to discover the origin of the concept as well as the origin of the recipe. I have seldom seen so much time spent on classroom work and energy put in searching for as many resources as possible!

Third, monitoring how the process towards goal realisation is going is a key aspect of self-regulated learning. Monitoring is also often called 'internal feedback' or reflection. As a learner, continuous reflection is necessary not only after action to evaluate its outcomes, but also during action, in order to be able to adjust it (Schön, 1983). Reflection-in-action is especially important because it allows adaptation of the actions in real time. However, it is hard to critically monitor your own blind spots. Therefore, feedback by relevant others is a valuable source of information through which a learner can confirm, add to, overwrite, tune or restructure his or her knowledge and strategies, cognitively, behaviourally as well as motivationally (Butler & Winne, 1995). However, one-third of all feedback interventions has negative effects on performance, so we should stress the fact that feedback has to be given in an effective manner (Kluger & DeNisi, 1996). Negative feedback in particular has potential detrimental effects when addressing the learner's self-concept. It can make the learner disengage with the feedback and reduce his or her self-efficacy. Therefore, if negative feedback is included, it needs to be formulated in terms of behavioural outcomes or the learner's action and not in terms of personality characteristics (Kluger & DeNisi, 1996). The next step is to use the learning goals resulting from the feedback to formulate an individual and group development plan that, in turn, is the basis for the next feedback session. For information on a model to integrate feedback in the workplace, see Besieux (2017).

Fourth, interaction with peers, teachers/trainers, coaches and experts about the learners' goals, their strategies to reach these goals and the results reached, helps the learners to become aware of strengths and weaknesses in how they regulate their learning process and supports them in findings ways to optimise. Moreover, modelling by experts has been shown to be a successful way of supporting learners in the development of self-regulated learning.

Finally, it is worthwhile to note that learner agency best resides in a safe climate: where it is safe to be yourself, safe to learn, safe to make mistakes and safe to acknowledge your own strengths but especially your weaknesses.

It is often argued that learner agency is quite problematic in business training for blue-collar workers, and even for high potentials, given they are often trained in learning settings where the teacher has full responsibility for the learners' learning. However, one should not always see agency as the transferring of full responsibility and steering. Gradually building learner agency might be the key to success, starting with the learner/employee understanding the goals and the relevance of the learning trajectory organised, reflecting on his learning process and outcomes, and eventually having openness and freedom in choosing some content and ways to learn. One step further is stimulating the employees to participate in designing their learning pathway, built on collaboratively discussed goals.

Alongside conditions that trigger and support learner agency, others potentially harm agency. For example, a high level of bureaucracy within an organisation hinders agency because of the formal regulation of learning. This limits the space for one's own initiatives, ideas and practices and therefore reduces autonomy over learning (Jones & Sallis, 2013).

Spark learner agency with the ABC for managers

Learner agency has to be learned and developed. When acting as a manager, you can facilitate this by using the ABC for people management. Martin Euwema, a colleague and professor specialising in organisational psychology, advocates that managers need to take the ABC of the manager into account seriously in order to become people managers. ABC stands for Autonomy, Belongingness (& Interrelatedness) and Competence. This stems from self-determination theory, where having autonomy, belonging to a group or organisation, and getting recognition for one's competence are stated as basic human needs. The more employees feel autonomous in planning their development, the more likely they will show persistent engagement to do so. The safer they feel in the team and the more recognition they feel they are receiving for their work, the more likely they will perform well.

Similar basic needs are at stake when we are learning. Getting some autonomy during our learning increases our motivation to engage; the feeling of belonging to a team results in us investing time and energy in what we do; and receiving recognition of our growing competences provides us with the courage to grow further. Research provides clear evidence that recognition leads to stronger self-efficacy, which is seen as one of the primary predictors of future learning (Van Dinther et al., 2011).

A vast amount of research has been conducted in finding out how these needs work in our daily lives. In the field of learning, some research has been conducted, but the practice of learning and instruction can still gain a lot in applying this know-how. Recognition or positive feedback is not yet an integral and daily part of coaching processes.

Recognition feeds our need for competence and this in turn feeds our engagement. Why would that be? If we experience that others value the work we do, we are likely to value our own work more and thus we are prepared to work harder for it.

Learner agency as leverage for learning and development

Organisations and companies should support learner agency to support L&D (Senge, 1990). But how difficult is that in business?

Learner agency is built by showing them how to see and support L&D relevance, helping them to understand the goal, supporting employees in reflecting upon what

TABLE 3.1

Learner agency is…

voice and choice
getting the power to create action
allowing engagement
seeing your own strengths and gaps
seeing and owning your next steps
knowing how to get there
effective feedback
learner responsibility
self-management

they do, and finally creating openness and freedom in choosing content and ways to learn. A next phase is to stimulate employees to participate and take responsibility in designing their own learning pathway. Some of these aspects build learner agency gradually in order to work towards building a learning climate in the organisation. And surely, learner agency best resides in a safe climate: by seeing your own strengths and your gaps (coached and facilitated by feedback), owning the next steps (taking responsibility, having autonomy) and knowing how to get there (facilitated by feedforward).

Building block 3: collaboration and coaching

Currently, in many organisations, working in teams is more and more integrated. So in our daily life, we do many things in teams or groups: working, dining, sports, travelling, etc. So what about learning in groups?

Some years ago I took part in a large meeting that ended with a dinner for participants. That is where I met Marijke, who told me that her utmost learning experience happened 25 years ago when she did a project with a small group over the course of 20 weeks. The learning experience was so profound that even 25 years later, she was still able to recall the content and the competences that she learned to an extent that was surprisingly detailed.

What is collaboration about?

Learning in well-coached teams brings you into a state of flow.

Over the past three decades, different forms of learning in groups have become popular instructional procedures in all levels of education and in most course subjects. In the same vein, organisations have become aware of the power of working in teams to enhance inter- and intrateam learning processes such as knowledge sharing and creating new knowledge together (co-creation of knowledge).

To date, in many universities, working in small groups has quite some history. In two of the five universities where I have worked, this has certainly been the case. At the University of Leuven we celebrate almost 50 years of project-based learning, which Professors Baert and Leirman started as an experiment in the late 1960s. Since it was founded in the 1970s, Maastricht University has been known for its problem-based learning approach where students work in small groups on authentic problems as the starting point for their learning process. In project-based learning as well as problem-based learning, the process of sharing and co-creating knowledge is at the heart of the teamwork. We have met many Leuven University graduates who have noted that what they remember from their training programme are those parts that they conducted with a small team. Many talk about the 'stickyness' of working together in projects or solving problems for real organisations. Even after 10 to 15 years they still know exactly what they did in the project and in the project team, how they coped with the problems they encountered and how much they learned about their field of study by cooperatively tackling the problem. The testimonial of a Maastricht University graduate discusses her experiences with the problem-based learning approach as follows:

> Being active in class seemed a lot easier in theory than it turned out to be in practice. But eventually I started to be more active in the tutorials. Even if I wasn't sure my contribution was going to be valuable, I'd speak up anyway. I'm no longer as shy and reserved as I once was; instead I've become more open and self-confident.
>
> *(Lisanly Vanblarcum, Curaçao, Master in Fiscal Economics[1])*

Teamwork is also implemented in organisations where innovation is a top priority, such as Spotify, Zappos, Google or Apple. Learning in groups is expected to boost knowledge sharing and co-creation of new knowledge to increase the overall capacity of the organisation to deal with the complexity of challenges and problems. The Service Science Factory is a good example of how to use team learning to boost innovation. The Service Science Factory helps businesses to identify and make tangible the challenges they face and the potential innovations to tackle them. In close collaboration with clients, they execute service innovation projects in which a new or improved service concept is developed by a team of academics, professionals and students with complementary relevant expertise, and coached by experienced project leaders. (If you want to know more about the Service Science Factory approach, go to www.servicesciencefactory.com/)

The key concepts in the field of group learning are collaborative and cooperative learning for educational settings and team learning for organisational settings.

The concepts of collaborative and cooperative learning are sometimes used as synonyms although clearly distinguished as different concepts by others. According to Bruffee (1995), cooperative learning is related to learning foundational knowledge (such as reading, grammar, history) and collaborative learning is related to non-foundational knowledge (such as critical argumentation and reasoning or construction of new knowledge). According to Panitz (1996), collaboration refers to a philosophy of interaction and personal lifestyle whereas cooperation is a way of organising learning through interaction in order to facilitate the acquisition of the learning goals. According to Dochy et al. (2014), in 'cooperative learning' settings, the learners split the work in order to work on the sub-tasks individually and bring all pieces together into the final output. In 'collaborative learning', ideas, knowledge, competences and information are shared to accomplish a task. Therefore, we prefer the term '*collaborative learning*': it stresses the interaction instead of the division of work in a small group (although many authors see collaborative and cooperative learning as synonyms).

TABLE 3.2

Collaboration is…

---

positive interdependence
peer interaction
accountable members
interpersonal skills
building knowledge (together)

Johnson, Johnson, and Stanne (2000) define *cooperative learning* in terms of five components. First, cooperative learning implies *positive interdependence*, which means that students perceive that the contribution of all group members is needed to reach the goal. Second, *peer interaction* is a core element. Although Johnson et al. explicitly mention this interaction to be face to face, current cooperative learning settings are in many cases hybrid or online. Third, the group can only achieve its goals if participants act as *accountable members*. Fourth, *interpersonal skills* (such as dealing with conflict) are needed to make cooperation effective. Cooperative learning practices give learners the opportunities to practise these skills. Fifth, cooperative learning implies different *socio-cognitive processes* such as construction of knowledge and co-construction of knowledge.

Collaborative learning can be organised in different ways such as peer learning and peer coaching. It is also one of the core elements of the instructional approach in project-based learning and problem-based learning. Each of these ways of organising collaborative learning has received considerable attention in the literature.

In his 2005 review, Topping defines peer learning as follows:

> Peer learning can be defined as the acquisition of knowledge and skill through active helping and supporting among status equals or matched companions. It involves people from similar social groupings who are not professional teachers helping each other to learn and learning themselves by so doing.
>
> *(Topping, 2005, p. 631).*

Peer coaching is defined as the process in which two colleagues engage in a mutually supportive relationship in order to enhance professional development. Peer coaching is implemented in schools as well as professional settings. The review studies by Ackland (1991) and the more recent one by Lu (2010) describe the different ways in which peer coaching is organised as well as the effects resulting from different studies. The characteristics and outcomes of problem-based learning have been reported in different review studies such as Dochy, Segers, Van den Bossche, and Gijbels (2003), Hmelo-Silver (2004) and Koh, Khoo, Wong, and Koh (2008). Helle, Tynjälä, and Olkinuora (2006) have published an overview of the literature on project-based learning.

Team learning

> *Team learning is the true motor in creating a learning organisation and a potential basis for continuous organisational growth and change.*

The term 'team learning' was introduced at the beginning of the 1990s with Senge's bestseller *The Fifth Discipline* (1990). Senge argued that team learning, rather than individual learning, is the true motor driving the creation of a learning organisation and a potential basis for continuous organisational growth and change. Team learning was further entangled by Decuyper, Dochy, and Van den Bossche (2010) who introduced the interdisciplinary approach, leading to the identification of eight team learning processes: sharing, co-construction and constructive conflict; team reflexivity, team activity and boundary-crossing; storage and retrieval. At the heart of team learning, we put the processes of sharing, co-construction and constructive conflict. Sharing refers to the process of communicating knowledge, insights, competences, beliefs, opinions or creative thoughts among team members. Co-construction takes the team one step further than sharing: they complement, confront and integrate each other's insights, competences, beliefs, opinions and creative thoughts. Constructive conflict refers to uncovering and integrating the diversity in identity, opinion, viewpoints etc. within the team through a process of negotiation or dialogue. For these basic team learning processes to result in improvement, facilitating processes are needed. Team reflexivity refers to the extent to which team members overtly and collaboratively reflect upon and discuss the team's objectives, strategies (e.g. decision-making) and processes (e.g. communication), and adapt them to current or anticipated circumstances. In addition, teams learn by collaboratively undertaking action which helps them to check their assumptions, their initially built shared understandings of a specific phenomenon. Finally, crossing the boundary of the team helps to open up minds again. Information, insights and critical reflections from different stakeholders such as clients or other teams help the team to fine-tune, deepen or broaden their thinking process. In this way, the processes of team reflexivity, team activity and boundary-crossing help teams to learn in the 'right' direction and therefore influence the efficiency and effectiveness of the team learning process (Dochy et al., 2014).

Storage and retrieval is about saving the newly developed insights in the software (collective memory) and/or the hardware (e.g. database or report) of the team, so that it can be retrieved and re-used in any later phase.

Team learning processes do not take place in a vacuum but are influenced by different interpersonal factors that emerge during the team process. We call these 'emergent states'. Teams learn and work in contexts that are shaped by these emergent states. I recently worked on an interdisciplinary project that aimed at developing new approaches to e-learning. Members with different backgrounds, experiences and stakes were involved. From the first minutes of the first meeting onwards, you could feel some vibration in the air: team members liked each other, they were happy to be in our team, they felt well, they strongly believed that this team would perform really well, the team was even able to cross any borders consisting of our restricted beliefs. And these beliefs did grow further in every meeting; they became stronger time after time when we were working together. This context pushed us further than we considered possible. This is how emergent states can work (or can hinder performance in some cases).

'Emergent states' that play a key role

We identified four emergent states that play a role: psychological safety, group potency and group efficacy, and team cohesion. Psychological safety is one example of an interpersonal belief that emerges at the team level and influences the extent to which the team engages in the aforementioned team learning processes. Edmondson (1999, p. 354) defines psychological safety as:

> a shared belief that the team is safe for interpersonal risk taking ... the shared sense of confidence that the team accepts someone for speaking up, even when his ideas or premature or controversory to other team members of current ways of thinking.

Not daring to speak up, because of being afraid of being rejected by other team members, is a very strong motive for team members not to share knowledge and not to participate in co-creation processes in the team. In addition, if you do not believe that this team might be successful, you will not put effort into any team learning process. This refers to the concepts of group potency and group efficacy. Group potency is the general belief that the team can be effective; group efficacy is the concrete shared belief that the team can do it, that it can be successful in finishing the task in hand. Team members that have a social and emotional bond are likely to put more energy and effort into the team process. Social cohesion refers to social and emotional bonds in the team, team members liking each other and caring for each other. Task cohesion implies that the team members are committed as a team to reach the team goal.

Our research, and that of many other researchers, time after time has added evidence to the key role of these 'emergent states' – a state that slowly builds itself as soon as the team gathers; the more the team works together, the further these states develop, or weaken. You might feel very safe in your team as soon as you meet, since you feel there is an emotional bond, a clique with the other members. After some work, there might be a weakening of this emotional bond since you might experience that your ideas are not appreciated or otherwise an increase if your ideas are exposed as excellent.

Why collaboration?

Research on learning in formal learning settings in the past decades has shown that *collaborative/cooperative learning* evokes clear positive effects in many ways. The different review studies (Bowen, 2000; Johnson and Johnson, 2009; Kyndt et al., 2013) are consistent in evidencing that students who work in collaborative learning settings outperform students in individualistic learning settings. More specifically, they outperform students in individualistic settings in cognitive and moral reasoning, time-on-task, long-term retention, intrinsic motivation and expectations for success, creative thinking, and transfer of learning. Moreover, students in collaborative learning settings showed more positive attitudes towards learning, the subject area and the training programme than their peers in individualistic settings. Positive outcomes are also reported at the relational level: in collaborative learning settings students showed more mutual liking and respect as well as providing more task-oriented and personal social support than their peers in individualistic settings. This seems to positively influence their social behaviour in the period after the collaborative learning. Also in terms of psychological health, Johnson and Johnson (2009) report positive findings:

> cooperativeness is positively related to emotional maturity, well-adjusted social relations, strong personal identity, ability to cope with adversity, social competences, basic trust and optimism about people, self-confidence, independence and autonomy, higher self-esteem, and increased perspective taking skills … commitment to one's own and others' success and well-being, commitment to the common good, and the view that facilitating and promoting the success of others is a natural way of life.
>
> *(Johnson & Johnson, 2009, p. 372)*

Our meta-analysis reported to what extent collaborative learning is effective for different study domains, age groups and cultures. The findings indicate that positive effects are larger for courses in maths and sciences than for social sciences. Also, youngsters up to 12 years and adults (18 years and older) profit more from collaborative learning in comparison to 12- to 18-year-olds.

With respect to collaborative learning in *problem-based learning (PBL) settings*, the results of review studies are comparable. The review by Dochy et al. (2003) was the first review searching for studies on PBL beyond the domain of medical education. The meta-analysis found that PBL has statistically and practically significant positive effects on students' knowledge application. Learners in a PBL environment show a slightly smaller knowledge base but in the long run remember more of the acquired knowledge, because they can rely on a more structured knowledge base (Dochy et al., 2003). A meta-analysis by Walker and Leary (2009) across 82 studies and 201 outcomes that crossed disciplines also favoured PBL compared to other approaches, as did several other reviews.

Studies reporting on *project-based learning* show that 'real assignment' work was found to be motivating. Learners reported that they had learned more or different issues compared to other courses, but also that the workload was high, partly because they did not have all the information they needed to solve the task right from the start.

Learners in project teams experienced a variety of positive outcomes: students learned much from the discussions within the project team; they learned from the peer assessment; they improved their communication skills and skills in analysing problems, and improved in developing, carrying out and monitoring plans; they learned to function in a team and to guide a team; they learned to apply theory in practice, to work independently and to monitor their own learning activities. Studies indicated that the intrinsic study motivation of students increased substantially during the project-based learning, and learners who were originally ranked lowest in self-regulation profited most in terms of intrinsic study motivation. Such learning prepares them well for their future work (Dochy et al., 2014).

During the past two decades, research on *team learning* has extended significantly. Many studies (e.g. Boon, Raes, Kyndt, & Dochy, 2013; Mathieu, Maynard, Rapp, & Gilson, 2008; Van der Haar, Li, Segers, Jehn, & Van den Bossche, 2015) have been evidencing in a persistent way the positive impact of team learning processes on task performance, the quality of intrateam relations, efficiency and innovativeness. Moreover, Van den Bossche, Gijselaers, Segers, and Kirschner (2006) as well as Boon et al. (2013) and Veestraeten, Kyndt, and Dochy (2014) found that merely gathering a number of people is not sufficient to create team learning behaviours, but that psychological safety, group potency, task cohesion, and interdependence were found to play important roles enabling team learning to take place.

How do you give feedback?

In addition to studies focusing on team learning processes, their outcomes and antecendents, research has been conducted to understand how team learning can be supported and enhanced. The review study of Gabelica et al. (2012) showed that, overall, giving feedback to the team does not only increase performance but also motivation and interest to work in the team and on the task, collaboration in the team as well as collective belief that the team is effective, in addition to increasing team cohesion and the expectation of positive outcomes.

However, positive effects are mainly dependent on how the feedback is organised. Accurate, timely, regular, non-threatening, shared, directly given and equally distributed feedback is effective. Positive feedback is generally more effective as regards increasing performance and improving the team process. Finally, feedback on the way in which the team is working on its tasks (process feedback) is more effective in driving team processes, while feedback on the results of the team process (performance feedback) triggers performance.

Team coaching

A jump towards coaching: Stop, look back, think, and plan forward.

In addition to feedback, different authors (Gabelica, Van den Bossche, De Maeyer, Segers, & Gijselaers, 2014; Konradt, Otte, Schippers, & Steenfatt, 2016) have stressed the importance of guided team reflexivity for enhancing team learning and in turn team performance. They argue that the learning potential of team feedback may not be realised unless teams actively process this feedback through the process of team reflexivity guided by a coach. This means stepping back from their team activity, reflecting on the past by taking into account the feedback received and deciding upon the next steps to take. The study by Gabelica et al. (2014) shows that combining team performance feedback and guided reflexivity leads to improved performance, even in the first phase of the team activity.

This brings us to the importance of coaching in collaborative and team learning settings.

Team coaching in collaborative settings

Coaching in collaborative settings refers to direct interaction with a team, with the intention of helping the team members to make 'coordinated and task-appropriate use of their collective resources in accomplishing the team's work' (Hackman & Wageman, 2005, p. 269).

Research (for example Stevens, Slavin, & Farnish, 1991) and our own experience in different settings have shown that for collaborative learners to remain focused on a task and on how they collaboratively process the task, support is needed. In project-based learning (starting from a larger project proposal, usually by an external party) as well as problem-based learning (starting from smaller problem descriptions), the role of the teacher (sometimes labelled as 'facilitator') is described as coaching, helping the group of learners to take the different steps in their collaborative learning process. The coach monitors and scaffolds not only the cognitive process of dealing with the task, but also the process of dealing with group processes. More concretely, the tutor's task is to stimulate and challenge students to critically question their thinking in order to further extend, modify or deepen their understanding; to monitor and stimulate so that all learners are actively involved in the group discussions; to monitor and provide feedback on the learning progress of the tutorial group as well as the individual learners; and to stimulate reflection in the group on their learning progress as well as interaction.

In organisational research, team coaching has recieved considerable attention. Team coaching has been defined as serving different purposes. First, it may have a motivational function, aiming to stimulate team members to act as a team, to avoid free-riding or 'social loafing' and to stimulate team cohesion (a shared commitment to the team and its task). Second, coaching may have a consultative function by addressing the performance strategy the team is using. This implies stimulating the team to critically reflect on the alignmemt of strategies and procedures used with the task requirements. Finally, coaching might have an educational purpose by monitoring and stimulating the contribution of each team member in order to make optimal use of the different expertise available and by stimulating team members to critically question and question each other's contributions (constructive conflict) in order to reach a team product that meets high-quality standards.

Hackman and Wageman (2005) argue that motivational coaching is especially effective during the start phase of the working team while consultative coaching is helpful when teams are at the midpoint of their performance period. We claim that educational coaching is important at all points in time. From the start onwards, valuing and using the unique expertise of each team member is essential in order to effectively start the work as well as to effectively progress.

In addition to the functions mentioned by Hackman and Wageman (2005), Edmondson (1999) has shown the importance of team coaching in terms of helping to create an environment in which team members feel safe to speak up, to not agree and to discuss divergent ideas. This belief of psychological safety enables team members to share knowledge, to discuss differences in views or perspectives, and to collaboratively create knowledge, which in turn fosters effective team performance.

In our own university programme, we implemented team-coaching to support project teams. More specifically, we used the principle of guided reflexivity. At the beginning of the project period, each project team is asked to formulate the five golden principles it believes are necessary for successful team collaboration. After two weeks each team member is asked to reflect individually on the golden principles: To what extent is the team working according to these 'principles'? Are all principles relevant? What critical events happened that might have caused negative tension in the team? How did you deal with them as a team? What positive flow did you experience as a team? What evoked this? To what extent do you feel your team reflects on the team cooperation during the project work? The individual reflections are put together anonymously in a team report that is sent to all team members and is inputted for a team reflection during an open office hour with the coach. The following questions are addressed: Are the five principles still relevant? Are any adjustments needed? As a result, the team can decide to reformulate the golden principles. The same procedure is repeated some weeks later: each team member receives an invitation for the individual reflection, and a collective team reflection (again focused on the five principles) is guided by the coach. After the closure of the project period, the students are invited for the final individual reflection. The team summary of the team results on the relevance of the golden principles is again shared and discussed during a team meeting with the coach.

Next to team coaching, in organisational management as well as learning science literature, the phenomenon of peer coaching has been subject to considerable interest. Peer coaching was first mentioned as a dimension of staff development for teachers (Joyce & Showers, 1980) and over the years it has been studied as well as applied in various fields such as counselling, nursing, medical education and professional development programmes for doctors, patient education.

In the management literature, it has been advocated as 'a powerful tool … [with] the potential to possess some remarkable properties: It can be high-impact, just-in-time, self-renewing, low-cost, and easily learned' (Parker, Hall, & Kram, 2008, p. 488). Peer coaching refers to the engagement of peers who are in many cases at

TABLE 3.3

Team coaching focuses on…

strengths of peers
dialogue on outcomes
reflection
self-evaluation
dialogue for inquiry and feedback

a similar level of knowledge 'in an equal non-competitive relationship that involves observation of the task, feedback to improve task performance and support in the implementation of changes' (Schwellnus & Carnahan, 2014, p. 39). In the management literature (Parker et al., 2008), it is stressed that a coaching process is about horizontal dialogue, focused on understanding each other's worldview and collaboratively reflecting on mental models, beliefs and assumptions. The dialogue is about planning and initiating learning opportunities and supporting each other in reaching the goals ahead.

Although various approaches to coaching exist, they have some characteristics in common. First, the focus is always on the *strengths of the peers* involved in the coaching process and on how to support the development of talents or competences. Second, at the start of the coaching, there is a *dialogue* between peers on the goals or preferred outcomes of the coaching process. Third, *reflection or self-evaluation* is part of the coaching process. Fourth, the *dialogue* between peers serves two purposes: *inquiry and feedback*. While the former aims to share information and insights about the coaching process, the latter refers to a dialogue where three questions are core: where am I moving towards? Where am I now? What are the next steps to take?

Recently, we explored 57 studies on team coaching (Barendsen & Dochy, 2017) and learned that facilitating the formulation of team goals is broadly seen as a leadership behaviour and responsibility, not primarily a coaching behaviour. This means that leaders and teams together formulate the goals they should aim at; a coach can play a role in stimulating shared commitment to these goals.

The study also revealed the most important and other relevant team coaching behaviours (Barendsen & Dochy, 2017): stimulating communication and shared commitment to the team goals, and the provision of encouragement and feedback were considered to be the most important for successful team coaching interventions. Also, the importance of team empowerment and encouraging team reflection was confirmed in our empirical study. The latter was rather perceived as a coaching behaviour that should be undertaken with teams that are further developed in their performance processes (more mature). Some coaching behaviours are considered to be closely interrelated; specifically, providing encouragement and feedback and enhancing interpersonal relationships were perceived as highly connected. Feedback was mentioned as requiring a level of trust, vulnerability and openness

TABLE 3.4

Effective team coaching interventions…

stimulate team communication	➢ Create an open, safe, and trusting atmosphere to share ideas and learn from each other;
	➢ Provide feedback on occurring team interaction processes and support the team to enhance the quality of their interactions.
build shared commitment	➢ Set clear expectations concerning team outputs;
	➢ Encourage collaborative efforts;
	➢ Stimulate team consensus on procedures and team goals.
provide encouragement and feedback	➢ Provide insight into the team's way of working and identify areas of improvement;
	➢ Encourage desirable performance behaviours;
	➢ Give recognition and praise.
enhance interpersonal relations	➢ Intensify interpersonal relationships;
	➢ Address conflicts and equip team members with conflict management skills for the future.
empower the team	➢ Empower by delegating tasks and dividing responsibilities among team members;
	➢ Give team members the opportunity to experiment and work out problems on their own, instead of immediately providing solutions;
	➢ Stimulate and encourage teams to coach themselves.

among team members and can in turn improve the interpersonal relationships within the team. In more concrete terms, these team–coaching behaviours focus on the aspects outlined in Table 3.4.

Overall, these coaching behaviours seem to work in 'situated coaching', meaning that behaviours can be more or less suitable depending on the team context and progression.

Success factors

What are the key success factors of peer coaching? Based on their review, Schwellnus and Carnahan (2014) distinguish eight success factors. First, mutual trust between peers is imperative and requires authenticity, for each person to be honest and open with him-/herself and their peers. Second, peer coaching needs to be voluntary, where both coach and coachee perceive mutual benefits of engaging in the coaching process. Third, although it is argued that feedback is an element of the coaching dialogue, coaching is effective when this feedback has a developmental and not an evaluative purpose. Fourth, feedback and reflection go hand in hand. Fifth, coaching that focuses on the strengths of the individual is more powerful than coaching that aims to define and work on the coachee's weaknesses. Sixth, effective coaching implies clear goals and working towards these goals. Seventh, coaching is dialogue so a coaching relationship is in nature cooperative. Eighth, whether the coach is a more experienced individual or a peer has no influence on the success of the coaching.

The benefits of peer coaching have been described in various fields of research and practice. Peer coaching results in an increase in competences, in being open to divergent views and in engaging in critical reflective dialogue, as well as giving each other affective or emotional support, which in turn made the subjects feel more comfortable and self-confident. Peer coaching has also been described as an effective tool in proactive career management. The study of Parker et al. (2008) indicated the following impacts: being capable of dealing with change; contribution to learners' professional growth; support for working on and reaching their personal and professional goals, including soft skills; an increase in self-confidence; a more accurate self-image; development of soft skills; empowerment; and an improvement in the skill of giving feedback.

Team coaching certainly indirectly contributes to team effectiveness and both directly and indirectly contributes to team innovativeness (Barendsen & Dochy, 2017). Moreover, it can lead to an increase in perceived efficiency and the team climate, and can help teams overcome several pitfalls common to working in teams. Compared to individual coaching, team coaching can have an increased impact on the level of change and development within organisations due to its systemic approach. It is, however, important to take into account the group dynamics, the developmental level of the team and the team's commitment during coaching processes.

Building block 4: hybrid learning

When television was introduced to the public, many thought that learning would change drastically. In schools, students were sitting in large halls to watch 'school television'. But it soon became boring, and evidence showed that television – just as the telephone, radio and computer – is a tool that supports learning rather than changing its core. This was very different when computers became connected to the internet. They were then more than a simple tool; there was a serious change in the availability and accessibility of information and so it brought more possibilities for variation (time, place, content). That fact also changed the essence of learning.

What is hybrid learning about?

Variation between online learning and offline face-to-face learning keeps the process going.

TABLE 3.5

Blended learning combines…

---

different media and tools in an e-learning environment
different didactic methods or approaches, such as instruction, video, group assignments, etc.
traditional learning and web-based online approaches
different modules into one programme
different modes of assessment

For many years, experts have understood that increasing variation in learning is one of the crucial factors for creating impact. As a consequence, they have promoted 'blended learning'. A major problem with blended learning is that it contains almost any form of blending: one can call using two different methods in one training programme 'blended learning' and one can also call the splitting up of learning content into two consecutive modules 'blended learning'. Also, using different media or blending modes of assessment or integrating the use of several social media platforms is seen as blended learning. It undoubtedly adds to increasing variation, but also adds to a terminological lack of clarity and it does not really promote the stronger sides of e-learning.

Looking then at what constitutes blended learning, one can conclude that currently all learning is blended since it is hard – if not impossible – to find a learning environment that does not meet any of the four modes above. Therefore, we argue in favour of the use of the term 'hybrid learning' when referring to a well-thought-out mix of online and offline learning methods.

> *All learning is blended learning; not all learning is hybrid.*
> *Hybrid learning is a well-thought-out mix of online and offline learning methods.*

'Online' means:

- using types of e-learning where teams of learners or learners and coach are present online at the same time such as live chat (text), video conferencing, web conferencing (learner is self-directed – synchronous (real time)) or at consecutive times (asynchronous) such as using discussion boards and other chat software;
- using the internet to find information, such as scrutinising a 'course library', searching and watching YouTube videos, searching databases, searching information on the web.

'Offline' refers to activities such as:

- working in face-to-face meetings;
- studying printed materials;
- writing a report;
- etcetera.

Hybrid learning is in the first place a more efficient use of available time: by preparing face-to-face meetings online, the meetings are more interactive and are constantly active, enabling a focus on knowledge sharing and collaborative sense-making.

Why hybrid learning?

MOOCs: we all talk about it; few do it; fewer persist.

Since e-learning only and using LMSs without learner marketing, offline meetings and support do not result in the desired impact, it is clear that hybridity is the only way forward.

The fact that e-learning, online learning, MOOCs (Massive Online Open Courses), etc. do not work as generally expected is mainly due to dropout.

Try to do the test yourself:

- subscribe to a MOOC and test yourself for how long you persist;
- test your colleagues or clients at your next training session, lecture or workshop: ask them who had subscribed to a form of e-learning course or MOOC and then ask how many of them finished the course. A few at best; usually no one!

This is in line with results from science, indicating huge dropout numbers: up to 95%.

Seaton, Bergner, Chuang, Mitros, and Pritchard (2014), for example, investigated 230 million student interactions and found that only 7% of the participants finished the course and that this 7% accounted for 60% of total time spent on the course. 76% of the participants merely browsed some materials, accounting for 8% of the time spent online. For MOOCs, the situation is not any better: out of 1 million students, only 4% completed the course (Cusumano, 2014). This is in line with other comparable findings.

E-learning on its own simply does not work at all.

What then does research show? Several studies and meta-analyses have shown mixed results about e-learning. Neutral or positive findings are only reported for some specific groups of people: for highly educated persons, with high levels of self-efficacy and with a clear learning goal orientation, e-learning seems to be as effective as classroom training.

Nevertheless, e-learning is not really successful at enhancing interaction (including peer interaction), at updating to recent know-how, and in its effectiveness of delivery (Carolus & Dochy, 2017). Frequently reported drawbacks are: poor interactivity, lack of feedback from the trainer and poorly structured synchronous sessions. And one should certainly ask: What does it matter if we know that only 5–10% of participants persist?

Looking at the current state of the art, there are arguments to state that online learning is probably not effective for any social skill. Moreover, online instruction can only be cost-effective if learners are also geographically very dispersed (Means, Toyama, Murphy, Bakia, & Jones, 2009).

Hybrid learning can be highly effective

Where, then, is the solution?

Studies comparing different training designs with the same group of learners on the one hand (such as Thai, De Wever, & Valcke, 2015) and reviews of research that analysed the effects of different variables in e-learning (such as Means et al., 2009) are both pointing in the same direction: hybrid learning.

The meta-analysis by Means et al. (2009) could not reveal whether some of the advantages of online learning conditions over face-to-face conditions were due to the online condition: *only and precisely hybridity (mixing online with face-to-face conditions) and the expansion of time spent on task had statistically significant effects.* Even the inclusion of media such as online quizzes did not increase effectiveness.

Hybridity can be underpinned by diverse types of evidence: Instructor involvement is proven to be a strong mediating variable; virtual teams that start with face-to-face meetings seem to outperform other virtual teams; hybrid trajectories are more effective than purely e-learning (Iverson, Colky, & Cyboran, 2005; Means et al., 2009; Sitzmann, Kraiger, Stewart, & Wisher, 2006; Zhao, Huang, & Lu, 2005).

Is there clear evidence of the effectiveness of hybridity?

First, over the past decades, at least 17 reviews have been published about the effects of combining online with offline learning, basically providing evidence that hybrid learning outperforms traditional offline face-to-face learning (e.g. Bernard, Borokhovski, Schmid, Tamim, & Abrami, 2014; Liu et al., 2016; Means et al, 2009).

The meta-analysis by Liu et al. (2016) shows that implementing hybrid learning in health professions results in a large and consistent positive effect on knowledge acquisition compared to a non-blended learning group. This means that hybrid learning settings are more effective than traditional face-to-face learning and pure e-learning settings. The authors of this review study explain the positive effects of hybrid learning as follows. First, compared with traditional learning, in hybrid learning settings learners have the possibility of reviewing online materials as often as necessary and at their own pace. This is likely to enhance learning performance. Second, in hybrid learning environments there are different triggers that interact with peer learners, which reduces feelings of isolation and at the same time helps the learner to stay on track and not to lose interest in the subject matter.

The review by Means et al. (2009) evidenced that in hybrid learning environments, K-12 learners performed on average higher than those in pure face-to-face instructional settings. In addition, spending more time on-task in the online condition increases the positive impact of hybrid learning. With respect to the use of tools such as online quizzes or other media, the studies reviewed do not support the assumption that they significantly enhance learning. For example, providing online quizzes does not seem to be more effective than assigning homework. Finally, giving learners control of their interactions with media and prompting learner reflection is important for effective online learning. Studies indicate that when students engage in online learning activities, this is more effective when learner activity and learner reflection are triggered.

Webinars should stimulate hybrid learning

Today, many educational institutions as well as L&D programmes in organisations make use of webinars. In this respect, research results demonstrate that web-based recorded short lectures are most beneficial when implemented in a hybrid context (where both traditional face-to-face meetings and fully online modes of learning are used) (Day, 2008; Day & Foley, 2006; Howlett et al., 2011; Lim & Morris, 2009; Owston, York, & Murtha, 2013; Taradi, Taradi, Radic, & Pokrajac, 2005). These studies use the term 'blended' to mean 'hybrid' (Garrison & Kanuka, 2004; Graham, 2006; Montrieux, Vangestel, Raes, Matthys, & Schellens, 2014). Face-to-face meetings combined with asynchronous communication tools (such as discussion forums) help the learner to discuss the information visited online and the knowledge developed with others as a way to adapt, fine-tune and deepen his/her own understanding. Hybrid learning, with the possibility of frequent face-to-face interactions, makes more deep and meaningful understanding possible.

In sum, while computers and software do not lead to more effective learning as a matter of fact, they provide many possibilities to make learning more attractive as well as being effective when thoughtfully combined with face-to-face interactions.

Second, using online learning opportunities makes engaging in learning activities more independent of time and place. Indeed, there are several logistic benefits in using hybrid learning. For example, the possibility of flexible scheduling increases engagement of the learner as he can undertake learning activities when needed and when feasable.

Third, hybrid learning, combining synchronous (online and offline) and asynchronous communication, results in increased interaction between learners and between learners and coaches and more open communication. This in turn results in higher levels of satisfaction, motivation and well-being of the trainees. The importance of interaction opportunities in blended learning settings is confirmed by a study by Lim, Morris, and Kupritz (2007). The results of this study show that, due to interaction opportunities in the hybrid environment, the learners reached a high level of understanding.

Fourth, the results of research studies show that when hybrid learning is implemented, there is a decrease in dropout rates. For example, Dziuban, Hartman, Juge, Moskal, and Sorg (2005) conducted longitudinal studies to measure course withdrawal rates in blended compared to online courses at the University of Central Florida. The results indicate that dropout rates on hybrid courses are lower than those in fully online courses. The authors argue that lower withdrawal rates can be explained by the support structure within the classroom. The face-to-face interactions reinforce the relationship-building between the teacher and the students, and offer the opportunity to make more explicit the expectations of the learning activities undertaken in the online learning environment.

Fifth, hybrid learning is an effective way of dealing with the problem of transferring what has been learned during a training programme to daily workplace practice. Research (e.g. Lee, 2008) has shown facilitating and hindering factors of online and offline learning to impact transfer of training: demonstration and activation through working online have a positive impact, while application is a facilitating factor when working offline. Moreover, hybridity can be crucial to transfer of training since it increases the impact of learning. Our own research demonstrated that a predictor of transfer of utmost importance is precisely the learning impact (Govaerts, 2017).

Given the aforementioned benefits of hybrid learning, one of the most important questions that training developers can ask themselves is: What is a good blend and how do you make one? Good hybridity is a mix of online and face-to-face methods and learning activities, in which the learner constantly and actively works with the learning content. The learner can do this individually or in interaction with the other trainees and the trainer. However, perfect hybridity does not exist. The optimal ratio between online and face-to-face learning is situation and context specific. Moreover, no one single medium has the best result for training and transfer. Instead, it is more the way in which media are used and the variation of media that is important.

At the organisational level, Dochy, Berghmans, Koenen, and Segers (2015) state that hybrid learning involves a fundamental reconceptualisation and reorganisation of learning and training, built on context-specific needs and characteristics. Furthermore, it is important for the organisation to make a good fit between the diverse HILL components and to integrate them. In this way, the organisation can create an ideal challenge for the trainees.

Certainly in the current era of learning from moving pictures, learning could be much better adapted to the new habits of the current generations. In this respect, hybrid learning is a response to the new needs of young people in schools as well as young employees. It aims to create a mix between online and offline learning and a wide variation in learning/training methodologies that can be used synchronously and asynchronously. Variation in instructional modalities, delivery media, instructional methods and web-based technologies contribute to hybrid learning since this variation is used to balance online and offline learning time. Due to this variation, the learner can create his or her own personal and unique learning path that ensures that learning becomes more interesting and effective.

The more variation in the methods used online and offline, the higher the motivation, engagement and impact.

Learners have needs; needs of feeling autonomous and happy. If we scrutinise literature on happiness, it is clear that there are some basic rules for increasing the time in which we feel happy.

First, increasing the frequency of enjoyable activities is more important than the quantity of happiness obtained. In recent years, we have spaced out weekend parties into smaller after-work parties; we space out long holidays into smaller weekend trips and short city trips.

In learning, small and frequent encouragement works better than giving one final score.

Second, variation in enjoyable activities avoids habituation. If you drink only top wines with great complexity and an outrageous bouquet, your feeling of consuming something really great and exceptional will fade away quickly. Wine lovers that drink both simple and complex wines do challenge themselves time after time to search for the ultimate sensory orgasm and to enjoy it, reflect on it, etc. For learning, varying encouragement and motivation approaches also work in a similar way, such as alternating oral encouragement with enjoyable activities such as a drink with the team, watching a weekly YouTube video of the week (selected by a rotating team member), a team-building outdoor activity, or a monthly fun hour organised by a team, etc.

Third, unexpected pleasures deliver a bigger thrill, as Friedman (2016) argued. Assume that you have a four-day city trip with your eight best friends. One (rotating) person organises this yearly. No one gets any information on where to go, how to go, what to wear, etc. One day beforehand you recieve an e-mail telling you what your suitcase should contain, where the meeting point is and what the dress code is: *Make sure you have summer and winter clothes with you, all in black; meet tomorrow at 6.00 at the Knightsstreet 1 and be dressed as a Gothic.* The next day, eight Gothics were transported to the airport for a surprise visit to the wonderful centre of Copenhagen. Do you think this works? I experienced it – surprises do work very well. For learning, varying enjoyment and encouragement also works: 'variation is the key of learning' (Prof. F. Marton, 1999).

Fourth, as demonstrated above, experiences enhance the feeling of happiness better and feel more rewarding than objects. A wine-tasting class is in most cases more rewarding than a plaque. Telling each other your experiences of progress, or what you are most proud of having accomplished since the last class, are useful experiences to share. Providing development opportunities that your workers can choose is more rewarding than a yearly flat fee that is taxed at high rates.

Recently, I was guiding a workshop for learning experts/coaches. I told them that I had recently learned to lime walls. I asked them to guess how I learned it. Almost immediately 95% of them said 'YouTube movies', which was correct. I also asked them how frequently they used YouTube in the learning activities they organise. While the answers were disappointing, at that time, two learners following a professional learning programme just peeped through the door of the workshop room. I waved at them and made signs that they were welcome to come inside to participate. They voluntarily entered the room, asking what was happening. After I explained that they had just entered a workshop for their trainers, I asked these trainees how many YouTube movies they watched daily. They answered, 'at least 10 and sometimes up to 20 or 30 per day'. When I asked them how many YouTube videos were used in their training programmes, they replied, 'none'. If we know that learning from video works well, that it adds variation, and that it brings the learning activities closer to your daily preferred activities, there is some food for thought. Why don't we use this more? Using YouTube and other videos is a way to add variation that is certainly adapted to the mindset of our millennials.

Building block 5: action and knowledge sharing

Consuming knowledge is not just like consuming food. In your favourite restaurant, nice dishes are served for you and you can relax and enjoy them.

Learning is different. Although information might be brought to you as a learner, turning this information into knowledge requires an active process in which the learner evaluates the new information by reflecting on it, using it to test its validity and discussing it with others. This is an essential step to connect the new information to what the learner already knows, to give meaning to the new information. Only then will it turn into personal knowledge, ready to use.

Stressing the importance of active learning, challenging and supporting students to do things and think about what they are doing, is not new. Already in the 1960s, Dewey argued for 'learning by doing'. Learners sitting back in their seats and consuming knowledge, skills and attitudes (KSAs) is ineffective. Since then, the plea for active learning has never disappeared. In the 1980s, experiential learning and action learning (Kolb, 1984; Revans, 1982) became popular. In the 1990s, 'constructivism' became a dominant paradigm in psychology and the learning sciences, and defined learning as involving the active construction of meaning by the learner. In more recent discussions on how to take into account the learning preferences of millennials, active learning has been put on the agenda of educators with urgency. It is argued that adopting instructional approaches based on the principle of active learning is critical in order to reach millennial students. Roehl,

Reddy, and Shannon (2013) describe these students as having been reared on fast-evolving technologies and as not accepting instructional approaches characterised by dissemination of information through lectures. They argue in favour of the flipped classroom as an example of an active learning pedagogy. In the flipped classroom model, students access information resources and work on new information at home, while classroom time is devoted to students working together on the information each of them brings in order to help each other in giving meaning to the new information. This implies a process of knowledge sharing. In sum, it is the combination of active learning and knowledge sharing that leads to growing insights.

What is active learning?

*When doing things and sharing know-how, you **'feel'** that learning is happening.*

Active learning is generally defined as any instructional method that requires students to engage in meaningful learning activities and reflect on what they are doing (Prince, 2004). Active learning is often defined by contrasting it to passively receiving information from an external source such as an instructor.

Two core aspects of active learning are learner agency (our first building block) and inductive learning processes (Bell & Kozlowski, 2008). First, as described earlier, agency refers to students taking responsibility for their learning process and controlling the learning decisions they take (which learning goals to go for, how to work on learning goals, monitoring progress, deciding on new learning paths to follow, etc.). In sum: internal regulation of the learning. Second, active learning involves inductive processes in which learners explore and experiment with a task in order to infer general concepts, procedures, rules and strategies that lead to effective performance. Key words are: exploring, experimenting, testing, (re-)formulating hypotheses, evaluating hypotheses, making errors and learning from them, planning, reflecting and monitoring. Examples of active learning approaches are: problem-based learning, case-based learning, cooperative/collaborative learning/teamwork; think-pair-share or peer instruction; conceptual change strategies; inquiry-based learning; discovery learning; and technology-enhanced learning (Michael, 2006). In these instructional approaches, active learning and knowledge sharing are two sides of the same coin. Learning is a process of linking practice to concepts through different iterations, and is created and further deepened through discussions and/or collaboration.

An interesting example is the Rich Environments for Active Learning (REALs) instructional system, which is promoted as an approach to engage learners in active learning via collaboratively building and reshaping knowledge through authentic experiences and interactions. Analysis, synthesis and solving of authentic problems, experimentation, and examination of topics from multiple perspectives are core activities, combined with knowledge sharing and building through collaborative learning in communities. The problem tasks that students deal with are authentic, which means they are realistic, meaningful, relevant, complex and information rich. Learner agency is stimulated and supported (Grabinger, Dunlap, & Duffield, 1997).

Another good example is the iSpot mobile app (www.ispotnature.org/) for crowd learning:

> iSpot is a website aimed at helping anyone identify anything in nature… Users post observations of nature to the site, by uploading photos of wildlife, logging where and when they saw it, and their guess at identification. iSpot aids identification by looking up scientific names from common names and checking the spelling with the dictionary of species. Other iSpot users – experts or beginners – can then 'agree' the identification if correct or provide an alternative identification if incorrect. A simple yet sophisticated reputation system gives feedback about expertise of users.
>
> *(www.open.ac.uk/iet/main/research-innovation/research-projects/ispot)*

iSpot is based on the principles of participatory active learning via social networking. Other interesting examples of crowd learning can also be found in other fields.

In the field of architecture, the 'Dynamic Architectural Memory On-line' platform for student and professional designers is an interesting example of how to encourage the exchange of ideas to improve building projects (Heylighen & Neuckermans, 2000).

Lessons from gaming: provide opportunities to grow, to be more competent and to regularly receive recognition for this.

Is gaming also action? Yes, it is. Games offer immediate feedback on performance and a sense of accomplishment when we succeed. If we break down gaming into a series of tasks at consecutive levels, we see that each of these tasks provides an opportunity to grow our competence and to receive recognition for this. In learning programmes, we should ask the following questions: Does every assignment provide the opportunity to grow, to be more competent and receive recognition for this? This can provide the energy to engage more and more. And growing engagement needs to be done contiuously, not at long-term intervals.

Why active learning?

Nobel Prize winner 2001, Carl Wieman (Stanford University) states that he collected over 1,000 scientific studies with students from diverse disciplines and diverse team sizes, all providing indications that such active learning principles consistently produce better learning results, less failure and advantages for all students, especially for students at risk. Wieman is certainly not the only one arguing against instructional approaches favouring passive learning, such as lectures. Based on a review of studies on expertise development, Elvira, Imants, Dankbaar, and Segers (2016) examined how to design a learning environment that supports the development from novice to professional expert. They argue in favour of two main design principles. First, give students access to a variety of authentic experiences combined with coaching including feedback and reflection to make explicit what is learned from these experiences. Second, support the explicit elicitation of knowledge via experiences through dialogue, discussion, and so on.

Over the years, many research studies have been addressing the effects of instructional or training interventions that are based on the active learning approach versus passive learning approaches. Let us summarise some of the main findings.

First, learners who engage in active learning outperform passive learners. This was confirmed in a meta-analysis by Freeman et al. (2014) including 225 studies and presenting comparatively the data on examination scores or failure rates of students experiencing traditional lecturing versus active learning in undergraduate science, technology, engineering, and mathematics courses. These results showed an improvement of average examination scores by about 6% in active learning settings while students in traditional lecturing settings were 1.5 times more likely to fail than the active learning students. This finding was consistent across the different courses.

In this respect, Deslauriers et al.'s study (2011) is interesting as it evidences the impact of the flipped classroom approach. They investigated two comparable groups of 250 learners in university physics classes, one group lectured by a strongly appreciated and very experienced lecturer, and the other groups working with an rather unexperienced teacher, trained in principles of active learning that are closely related to the HILL approach. The latter means that this group used a pre-class reading assignment (four pages), pre-class quiz (short online quiz), in-class clicker questions, and more importantly student–student discussions, small-group active learning assignments and continuous feedback during meetings. After three meetings of the same duration for all groups, using the same goals, the same tests were administered to both groups directly after the third lecture/meeting. The active groups (mean score 74%) outperformed the lecture group (mean score 41%).

We should note that the type of examination or assessment used affects the extent to which active learners outperform passive learners. For example, in their study, McKeachie, Pintrich, Lin, and Smith (1986) found no differences between lectures and discussion methods for the memorisation of lower-level factual content. This is in line with our earlier study about the effects of problem-based learning (see the review by Dochy et al., 2003). However, several studies found that lectures were less effective for the long-term retention of knowledge, the application of knowledge to new contexts, the development of higher-order thinking, attitude change and motivation (see also Pascarella & Terenzini, 1991 and McKeachie et al., 1986).

Second, learners who are stimulated to explore and experiment, as opposed to being spoon-fed instruction, are better able to use their newly developed insights to deal with and work on new tasks, the so-called transfer of learning (Bell & Kozlowski, 2008).

Third, active learning implies making errors and learning from them. Ample research has confirmed the impact of having the opportunity to make errors as a learner and of being supported in how to turn the error into a learning experience (Bell & Kozlowski, 2008). It is a key success factor in developing into a so-called adaptive expert, a professional who combines occupational expertise with a high level of flexibility to deal with the new challenges he or she meets.

Fourth, learners who frequently engage in active learning experience how they continuously gain knowledge and insights. This experience of growing and developing is personally rewarding and motivates them to take the next steps, to walk the extra mile, to persist when hurdles have to be taken. Braxton, Milem, and Sullivan (2000) have evidenced that supporting active learning influences the learner's persistence in engaging in learning, growing and developing. Moreover, active learning with sharing knowledge as a crucial lever brings learners together, stimulates them to become part of a learning community and subsequently to stay in the programme (retention decision).

Then, when can we still lecture?

Mulryan-Kyne (2010) and others have shown situations where 'lecturing' is still appropriate and state that critics on lectures come from 'inappropriate use' and certainly the 'overuse' of them.

Lecturing is only appropriate:

(1) When information is not available in an accessible way (Does this still happen? Information is mostly accessible; although we are not sure it is relevant and reliable, but that is exactly what we have to teach people)
(2) When it is necessary to introduce an assignment
(3) When you want to show and explain alternative views as preparation for discussion or assignments
(4) When 'extra' explanation is asked for, preferably just-in-time.

Speech is bronze; sharing is silver; constructive conflicts are gold.

Employees prefer to learn from peers; students learn from peers – sometimes more than from experts.

When I discussed the criteria for evaluation with my students, I was scared that they would turn up with nonsense criteria. They never did. The criteria they proposed were often close to the ones on my list of rubrics. When I discussed an additional criterium on my list, after some closer explanation learners usually agreed fully. When they had additional criteria resulting from their brainstorming, I felt quite ashamed that I had not come up with such obvious criteria. Usually, it seems as if we cannot phrase such criteria any more due to too much expertise. For example, some steps in problem-solving become so obvious to experts that they do not make them explicit any more when asked how they solve such a problem. Ericsson's (2016) research on expertise and deliberate practice confirms this.

Sharing between workers, learners, students and employees is still an underestimated act that stimulates learning. And sharing is, of course, a necessary condition to arrive at construction of knowledge, co-construction and constructive conflict.

Sharing of information is of great importance to teams as it positively influences team performance (Boon, Vangrieken, & Dochy, 2016). When sharing of information develops into the collaborative building of new knowledge, we speak of co-construction. Learners that discuss information, build on it, reason on it, improve, adapt and combine it, can eventually create new knowledge, ideas, arguments, etc. (Boon et al., 2016).

> *Constructive conflict takes learners out of their comfort zone.*

During the sharing of information and of personal understanding and opinions about it, cognitive conflict or controversy can arise when learners express different understandings. Constructive conflict can, by taking the team out of its comfort zone, lead to discussion, exploring different views, deeper understanding, error analysis, insight, and even drastic transformations.

There is no doubt that having constructive conflict in teams (or dyads) is the driver of team learning. Constructive conflict (also called constructive controversy by Johnson & Johnson, 2009), stimulates deepening knowledge and insight. Many times this finding has been the core message of research on learning in teams that we and our colleagues conducted (e.g. the research by Edmondson, Van den Bossche, Raes, Boon, Van der Haar, and others).

Cognitive conflict can be constructive, motivating people to seek new knowledge, to learn about the perspectives of others. Constructive controversy involves deliberative discussions that can emerge in creative problem-solving. Johnson and Johnson (2009) entangled the basic process behind constructive controversy. When learners are confronted with a problem, they search for information (today usually in a 'bitty' manner) and form a preliminary solution or hypothesis. When confronted with peers' differing hypotheses, theories and findings, they become

TABLE 3.6

Constructive controversy leads to...

greater mastery and retention of the subject matter
higher-quality problem-solving
greater creativity in thinking
greater motivation to learn more about the topic
more productive exchange of expertise among group members
greater task involvement
more positive relationships among group members
more accurate perspective taking
higher self-efficacy
greater joy in learning

uncertain of that initial solution. This trigger motivates learners to search for more information and better arguments or more convincing evidence. This effort yields creative solutions and creates joy and engagement, sometimes leading to a state of 'flow'. Hence, participants also learn to criticise ideas not people, and to take on board another's perspective. Working with constructive conflict leads to more effective sharing of expertise, and in the long run, learners undergo a lasting change of attitude. Moreover, learners develop a stronger sense of mutual friendship and support and are more able to cope with stress and competition. Johnson and Johnson summarised the benefits of constructive controversy (see Table 3.6).

In sum, the 'sharing through action' HILL building block refers to learners collaboratively building knowledge and developing understanding through active involvement. This implies that learning takes place just-in-time, when there is a task to do or a problem to solve. Involving learners in action creates opportunities to make mistakes, get immediate feedback and learn from it. Active learning in a hybrid learning environment gives room for engagement in learning by doing it at a time and place most convenient to the learner.

Building block 6: flexibility – formal and informal learning

How many great things did you learn outside the walls of a school or training room? Surely many. I learned many things – varying from riding a bike to laying bricks and using apps and software in everyday life – unplanned, without structured guidance, without clearly stated goals, and not at any planned time or location.

I remember that my father explained to me how he learned his competence as an entrepreneur, including competences in accounting, marketing, and managing his teams of workers at the workplace. My grandfather started an industry in glass and mirror production after World War II. My father, after studying in Brussels, was dropped in the firm as CEO and learned day after day, mostly unplanned, without stated goals, triggered by everyday challenges.

What is flexibility with a mix of formal and informal learning?

When your own learning track is flexible, not overloaded, and providing both spaced informal moments and formal training; you will actually start to like learning.

Flexible learning implies that employees have the opportunity to grow and develop by participating in formal training programmes as well as by learning how to deal with new questions, challenges and problems as part of everyday work, mostly referred to as informal learning.

Formal learning is learning that is planned. It is a method of learning that is often used in the workplace and in corporate settings. There are different forms of formal learning to distinguish, such as web-based learning, learning through a structured lesson, or learning planned outside the workplace. When formal learning takes place in the workplace, it is usually positive for the organisation since participation in the training programmes is significantly and positively related to the individual's job performance (Morin & Renaud, 2004). However, there is ample evidence that, in order to create impactful training programmes, careful design is necessary. The building blocks described in this book describe which aspects to take into account when designing a formal training programme. Moreover, one must remember that formal learning in different work situations is usually not good enough when one takes all the changes and challenges in the workplace into account (Svensson, Ellström, & Åberg, 2004). Therefore, it is not only important for formal learning to take place, but also informal learning.

In recent years, many discussions have suggested that informal learning is a kind of 'hidden potential' for people to learn. Many experts agree on the large value of informal learning at work or 'everyday learning'. We feel that learning during your everyday activities is indeed valuable, but it is not necessarily cheaper than other forms of learning. The reason for this may be clear: informal learning can only appear when is it sufficiently facilitated by the creation of favourable conditions for learning. These favourable conditions do usually not come by themselves, but cost effort, time and money.

How does informal learning in organisations work?

Employees learn at work through problems, errors, questions, changes, critical incidents, challenges, and so on in the work itself; these are often called triggers and add to future performance improvement. Such triggers can be different challenges to approach content in a better, more profound or different way (see the following examples from Baert).

Baert (2017) gives the following examples of such triggers: rapid changes in the technologically driven environment, collaborative and innovative work structures, flatter organisations, strong relationships with clients who increasingly seek input into design of products and services, and more flexible partnerships with suppliers for rapid, lean, just-in-time production and delivery.

These triggers have been slowly influencing organisations' human resource management (HRM) systems. Based on a literature review, Soderquist, Papalexandris, Ioannou, and Prastacos (2010) argue that current 'HRM processes need to be centred on the flexible and dynamic deployment of employees' competences, rather than on task-related and pre-defined sets of qualifications, as traditionally has been the case' (p. 326).

> Today, the key question refers to the competences that superior performers possess in order to successfully execute a range of activities (e.g. in projects, inter-functional teams, or problem-solving task forces). In this context, competences differ from KSAOs (Knowledge, Skills, Abilities, and Other characteristics) in that they shift the level of analysis from the job and its associated tasks, to the person and what he or she is capable of.
>
> *(Soderquist et al., 2010, pp. 326–327).*

The transition from job-based HRM systems to competence-based HRM systems has been reinforcing the re-conceptualisation of L&D in organisations. It is argued that L&D practices should encompass a wider variety of learning opportunities for employees than traditional training and development programmes (e.g. Manuti, Pastore, Scardigno, Giancaspro, & Morciano, 2015). It has put the combination of formal training programmes and opportunities to learn as part of everyday work, informal learning, on the agenda.

It is clear that everyday problems and challenges are strong triggers for learning and that having opportunities to engage in informal learning activities will satisfy the urgent need and curiosity better than subscribing to a formal training programme.

But what is informal learning precisely about and how is it different from formal learning?

The core idea of informal learning is that people learn from their experiences when they face a novel challenge. Given that their current understanding is not sufficient to deal with the challenge in an effective way, they have to look for alternative ways of interpreting and analysing the situation. In turn, they require novel responses. A critical reflection on the results of using these novel responses in work practice leads to new insights that can be used when addressing novel problems in the future (Watkins & Marsick, 1992). Figure 3.1 compares the characteristics of formal and informal learning on five continua.

The first continuum refers to the degree of structure in terms of planning and organisation of the learning content, support by others, time, and objectives. Informal learning activities are characterised by a lower degree of structure than formal learning activities (Kyndt & Baert, 2013). Informal learning implies that the learner engages in learning content he or she needs in order to solve an issue at hand (e.g. a problem or question he or she faces).

Formal learning	Informal learning
High degree of structure	Low degree of structure
External validation	No external validation
Classroom setting	Workplace setting
Trainer controlled	Learner-controlled
External stimulus	Internal stimulus

FIGURE 3.1 Formal and informal learning defined on five continua

The second continuum reflects the difference between formal and informal learning in terms of validation (Noe, Tews, & Marand, 2013). While formal training programmes lead to a certificate, this is not the case for informal learning activities. Over the past few years, validation of informal learning has become a key concern in EU lifelong learning policies. The acknowledgement that learning takes place in a variety of settings – including outside of classrooms – has led to a plea for making visible 'the entire scope of knowledge and experience held by an individual, irrespective of the context where the learning originally took place' (Colardyn & Bjornavold, 2004, p. 69). However, by organising a validation process, part of the informal learning process, more precisely the assessment of the outcomes of the informal learning activities, becomes formalised.

The third continuum refers to the physical place where learning takes place. While informal learning takes place in the workplace, integrated into daily work life, formal learning takes place in face-to-face or virtual classrooms.

The fourth continuum represents the locus of control of learning, with more learner control in informal than in formal learning activities. That is, much more than in formal learning, in informal learning the when, what, how, and why to learn primarily depend on the learner's choice and motivation (Noe et al., 2013).

The fifth continuum refers to the stimulus for learning, which differs significantly between formal and informal learning. While in formal learning the stimulus for learning is mainly external – that is, set by an instructor or a curriculum – in informal learning, learning is primarily triggered by an internal stimulus that signals dissatisfaction with the current ways of acting or thinking (Marsick & Watkins, 2001; Noe et al., 2013).

By describing the key features of formal and informal learning on these five continua, we acknowledge that many learning activities can be described as partly formal and partly informal. An example is described by Tynjälä (2008), who refers to Poell's (2006) model of learning projects. In learning projects, participants intend to learn and improve their work at the same time. The learning projects are organised by a group of employees and originate from a work-related problem. Employees participate in a set of activities which are centred on the work-related problem and take place in different kinds of learning situations, that can be both on-the-job and off-the-job, self-organised and facilitator-/instructor-directed, action-based and reflection-based, group-focused and individual-oriented, externally and internally inspired, as well as pre-structured and open-ended.

Although formal and informal learning are described as different ends of continua, they can be complementary. That is, formal training programmes can be accompanied by informal learning activities (e.g. discussions during breaks) and informal learning activities may lead to the need to participate in formal training programmes (e.g. when feedback-seeking leads to the identification of gaps in skills which may be most efficiently addressed by participating in formal skills training).

In addition to the different continua helping to describe work-related learning activities as being more or less formal or informal, different authors have identified different types of informal learning which result from different characteristics of the learning activities and the setting at hand.

First, with respect to the intention to learn, Eraut (2004) distinguishes between deliberate, reactive, and implicit informal learning activities based on the level of consciousness and goal-directedness of learning. Implicit learning is a totally unconscious learning process in which the learner does not recognise either that he or she has been learning or what has been learned. While informal learning is hardly ever fully implicit, it is also quite likely that explicit forms of informal learning have some implicit aspects. For example, by writing this HILL book and rechecking the literature resources, I have deepened my own understanding of the building blocks, although this happens quite unconsciously. Reactive learning refers to learning activities that are near-spontaneous such as reflection on past experiences, noting facts, asking questions, and observing the effects of actions. It involves a more conscious and intentional effort to learn. For example, when a new product or service is explained to a client, the client's questions trigger the developer to reflect on different aspects of the product or service in order to look for optimisations. The developer learns by reflecting on and dealing with the client's questions. Deliberate informal learning means that there is a clear work-based goal that leads to learning activities. Learning in the sense of individual professional development is a probable by-product of these activities. Deliberate learning involves activities that are part of daily work such as discussing and reviewing past actions and experiences, engaging in decision-making, and problem-solving.

Second, a distinction is made between individual informal learning activities and informal learning in social interaction (e.g. Kyndt & Baert, 2013; Mulder, 2013). According to Noe et al. (2013), individual informal learning includes learning from oneself and learning from non-interpersonal sources while informal learning in social interaction includes learning from others. Learning from oneself refers to reflection and experimenting with new ways of thinking and acting. Learning from non-interpersonal sources implies retrieving information from written material (e.g. via the internet). And learning from others involves interaction with peers, supervisors and relevant others in the learner's network by seeking information, help or feedback, or by exchanging ideas and discussing the problems at hand.

How to foster informal learning: the role of the organisation

Informal learning is regulated by the learner and under his or her responsibility and control. Does this imply that the organisation has no role and does not need to invest in informal learning? No, on the contrary, the organisation plays a crucial role in creating the conditions that foster informal learning. These conditions concern the extent to which certain activities are part of the culture and mindset in the organisation, such as acting upon professional discussions, feedback, collaborative conversation, being observed and receiving feedback, proactively seeking information and seeking help (Baert, 2017).

I remember my visit to a large IT multinational. On the agenda was the discussion of how to enhance knowledge exchange in the R&D department in order to increase time-to-the-market. Before we started the meeting, I walked with an L&D officer to the coffee corner to get a cup of coffee. She told me that the company had decided to remove all coffee corners as they perceived the chats in the coffee corner as a waste of time.

What are the stimulating conditions to create when you want to foster informal learning?

Many scholars have been talking about instilling a learning climate as the umbrella concept for conditions that foster informal learning (Emonds, Dochy, & Segers, 2017). What are the core dimensions of a learning climate?

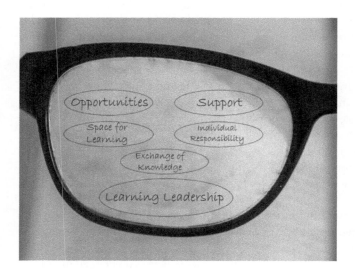

FIGURE 3.2 A climate for learning – components (Emonds et al., 2017)

First, opportunities to learn: Are you giving your workers opportunities to develop and grow? Are there ways to access and share information and are you giving them time and space to connect to others and collaborate?

Second, support: Is there explicit recognition, rewarding and approval of learning behaviour by supervisors as well as colleagues; is learning facilitated? These questions refer to task-related support. In addition, support is needed on the socio-emotional level. Is there a climate of trust and warmth among colleagues and supervisors? Is there psychological safety when you're talking about learning? Do people trust their coworkers/managers enough to firmly state their opinions without repercussion? Is there room for making mistakes, sharing them as a first step to reflect on them and learn from them? Is there room for critical questions?

Third, space for learning: Is there a space for learning within your company? What structures are there in place in your company when it comes to learning? Are there any constraints that people will be facing? Are you giving your people time to learn and is there explicit awareness of time constraints?

Fourth, individual responsibility: Are you allowing and trusting people to take responsibility in decision-making processes? Is there a role clarity that can support them in making decisions about their learning? Is there minimal regulatory guidance and control and maximal dialogue and initiative?

Fifth, exchange of knowledge: We separated this dimension from the dimension of 'opportunities' since you can create opportunities within your company, but that doesn't mean that there is actually exchange of knowledge taking place at those times. When we talk about exchange of knowledge, we talk about the attitudes towards dialogue and conflict. How do people talk to each other? Are they seeing learning opportunities in failure? What is their dialogue like when it concerns learning? Are they having constructive or deconstructive conflict, relational conflict or task-related conflict?

Finally, the sixth dimension is also the most important one and could even be described as the basis of all the others: learning leadership. Are your leaders facilitating learning behaviour and supporting it in their daily life? Are your learning leaders promoting innovation and risk-taking? Are the results of innovation and risk-taking shared and discussed? Are the leaders an example of learning while working, for example by sharing critical experiences and proactively seeking feedback themselves? Do they create time for analysis and reflection? Do they provide constructive feedback on a regular basis? Do they promote teamwork? Do they appreciate and support efforts to learn? Do they provide feedback and rewards for proficiency? Do they stimulate and reward learner agency? (Kyndt, Govaerts, Smet, & Dochy, 2017)

Parallel and even inherent to building a learning climate, some job and work arrangements are important levers for employees to engage in informal learning.

First, think about how to organise work so that employees do not end up in only routinised activities in which there are no triggers to learn. Involving employees in task forces, project groups, and so on opens up for them a world of problems never experienced or thought about before: of making errors if the problem is quite wicked and/or relevant prior experiences are lacking; of critical incidents, challenges, and so on. For employees, this means that they encounter challenging tasks as well as, or as a consequence of, work and job variety (Kyndt et al., 2017).

Second, and related to the condition of challenging tasks, empirical evidence suggests that experiencing a heavy workload enhances informal learning. However, there are two points of attention. First, when the workload becomes too high, a lack of time will hinder employees from engaging in learning. Second, a heavy workload, combined with a feeling of not being under control with respect to tasks and timing, will result in less investment in learning (Kyndt et al., 2017).

Third, create structural opportunities for communication, interaction and cooperation within your own organisation. This implies making information from inside and outside the organisation accessible, fostering communication between all units of the organisation, and making explicit time and space for social contact among employees (Kyndt el al., 2017). Concrete examples of how to make this happen are: organise regular meetings where units can consult with each other; use trade union meetings as learning opportunities for the participants; share internal job openings, stimulate job rotation and organise common breaks (Baert, 2017); plan how to onboard new employees; think about the architecture of the workplace in terms of proximity and therefore easy accessibility of colleagues, rooms for teams to meet and so on (Kyndt et al., 2017).

Fourth, enhance participation in internal and external networks. Possibilities are: organise teamwork; implement intervision; organise debriefings to reflect upon and learn from projects and activities; share rooms to confer; plan meetings with external colleagues and visits to other organisations; invite guest speakers; organise communities of practice with external partners (Baert, 2017). Organising teamwork is, of course, one of the most obvious ways to give employees the opportunity to develop a network in and from which he or she can learn. Further information on the conditions that need to be in place for teamwork to act as a place where learning with and from each other is inherent to the work can be found under the building block 'collaboration'. Just to mention two points. First, diversity and complementarity in teams trigger team members to open their eyes and mind more to the expertise of others than is the case in homogeneous teams. Second, given that the responsibility for process and product is high in self-directed teams, the urgency to build upon each other, so as to learn from and with each other, is strong.

Fifth, create opportunities for feedback and reflection, for example: by using PDPs (personal development plans); implementing a buddy system or godfather/godmother system; introducing coaches and/or mentors; introducing internships so that new ideas flow into the organisation which trigger employees to reflect; introducing career consultation (Baert, 2017).

Sixth, increase the access to information and databases or systems by providing a newsletter; access to databases; promoting an idea box; providing access to a quality manual (Baert, 2017).

Also on the strategic level, conditions can be created to foster engagement in workplace learning (formal as well as informal). In this respect, the concept of Strategic Human Resource Management/Human Resource Development (SHRM/D) is often used. The importance of linking L&D practices and policies with the strategy to foster flexibility and, therefore, pave the way for organisational change is widely recognised, bringing HR departments to the forefront of organisational transformation (Truss & Gratton, 1994). In this respect, the concept of Strategic HRM (SHRM) has been put forward. SHRM is the practice of aligning and integrating HRM policies and practices with the overall business strategy, so that the organisation's human capital can most effectively contribute to its strategic business objectives (Cascio, 2015). SHRM implies not only linking HR practices with the organisational strategy but also linking the practices themselves to ensure that they are promoting the same goals (Truss & Gratton, 1994). This also applies to Human Resource Development (HRD): the role of L&D needs to be strategic, indicating the necessity for L&D policies and practices to be aligned with the business strategy by assessing the current capabilities, what is needed and what will be needed in the future (Panda, Karve, & Mohapatra, 2014). Alignment is a process of interaction between the key players in the organisation at different levels. It is based on the existence of clear communication and mutual understanding of the vision and the strategy at all levels of the organisation. Communicating and sharing strategic information, however, can be extremely challenging considering the number of employees required to carry it from and to different levels of an organisation. In addition to alignment, engaging in workplace learning, in terms of formal as well as informal learning, becomes important in the eyes of the employee and becomes a inherent element of daily work only when the organisation recognises and rewards investment in learning.

I remember an organisation where it was decided to change the form of the yearly performance appraisal interviews, by literally giving more space for describing the needs and activities for further development than for reporting on past performance and achievements. The aim was to recognise the importance of learning. A few years later, it was decided that the section on Professional Development only needed to be filled in by employees with a tenured term. The signal was clear: L&D is of no value for fixed-term employees.

Why a well-thought-out mix of formal and informal learning?

In general, it is argued that learning at work may be of benefit to both the organisation and to the career of the employee (Baert, 2017; Kyndt et al.,2017). Svensson et al. (2004) claim that the integration of formal and informal learning is necessary for better employee competences and organisational productivity.

Is there any evidence for this claim?

Previous research has consistently evidenced that the learning gains of formal training programmes are usually weaker than we think. Of course, what's in a word? Training is a must and if we include HILL building blocks, impact will rise.

Many review studies on transfer of training, examining whether participating in a training programme leads to the use of the newly acquired knowledge, skills and attitudes during daily work, yielded disappointing results. Most formal training programmes seemed not to be designed in such a way that transfer is enhanced. This is precisely one of the reasons why we have decided to develop the HILL model.

Therefore, during the past decade, we have been conducting several studies aiming to unravel the unique contribution of formal and informal learning to employees' professional development.

Our study (Gerken, Beausaert, & Segers, 2016), conducted in a university setting, questioned the extent to which the formal and informal learning of faculty staff was related to the employees' employability. Formal learning referred to participating in formally organised L&D activities (training programmes, workshops, lectures). Informal learning was described as engaging in three proactive social informal learning behaviours, namely help-seeking, feedback-seeking, and information-seeking. Employability was measured in terms of three competences: occupational expertise, flexibility (reacting to changes and challenges) and anticipation of changes and challenges (Van der Heijde & Van der Heijden, 2006).

The results indicated that social informal learning relates to employability. More specifically, seeking feedback and more concretely acting upon the feedback generated from colleagues, as well as external information-seeking, supported faculty staff to anticipate future changes and act upon them. In addition, seeking help from others helps them to be flexible when meeting challenges in their daily work and to react to them in an effective way. On the contrary, our data did not show any influence of engaging in formal learning on faculty staff's employability.

Another study (Froehlich, Beausaert, & Segers, 2017) was conducted in three different organisations: a university (including faculty staff as well as administrative staff), a Chamber of Commerce and an IT company. The findings show that formal and informal learning have a differential effect on employability. More specifically, engaging in formal learning affects the extent to which employees anticipate challenges and changes ahead and react accordingly. With respect to informal learning, we see a stronger as well as a broader impact on employability. Employees who engage in information- and help-seeking indicate a higher level of expertise in their occupations, being more able to passively (flexibility) as well as proactively (anticipation) deal with challenges and changes ahead. In sum, information- and help-seeking contribute in many ways to employees' employability. Feedback-seeking serves a more unique purpose: it helps to anticipate changes ahead.

In sum, the finding that formal learning is only supportive at being able to anticipate challenges and changes ahead might indicate that formal learning activities are especially well suited to learning about new domains. Informal learning, supporting occupational expertise, flexibility and anticipation, may subsequently be efficient for further developing competences.

These results show the value added by formal and informal learning, although there are differences between organisations. As far as we know, there is not yet evidence on the exact ideal distribution of formal and informal learning activities.

Building block 7: Assessment as Learning

If you get frequent feedback and assessment that is either used as a start or as a way of monitoring what you do; your drive to learn will thrive.

Assessment is the act of collecting and interpreting information about the learner's learning process and performance. The learner gets to know whether and how they have made progress, how far they are in the developmental trajectory towards their goals and their needs in terms of the next steps to take. In addition to the powerful role of assessment in informing the learner on steps to take in the L&D trajectory, assessment also, often implicitly, steers the learner's learning behaviour. There is ample evidence that learners interpret assessment practices as signals of what is important according to the teacher or supervisor. Learners tend to adjust their learning behaviour to the method of evaluation used or the content being assessed.

This is the reason why if we aim for High Impact Learning we should consider very carefully how to use assessment: alignment of the assessment practices with the learning and support process is of crucial importance.

A few years ago, we interviewed middle managers and employees in a large multinational company using portfolio assessment. We were interested in the purpose for which the portfolio assessment was being used. The HR department as well as the middle managers communicated that the purpose of the portfolio assessment was developmental, supporting the employees in exploring strengths and weaknesses in their competences as input for deciding on next steps to take in the developmental trajectory. Employees, however, were explicitly expressing their opinion that the portfolio assessment served multiple purposes. The information from the portfolio (strengths and weaknesses) was not only used for discussing next steps in the L&D trajectory but was also then used as input for high-stake decisions such as promotion, salary, and so on. As a consequence, employees were not very eager to reflect on their professional development in an open and honest way. They admitted to the interviewer that they played the game, given that you were never sure when and how your reflection would be used 'against' you.

This example shows the powerful role that assessment practices play and consequently the importance of a carefully designed assessment practice. If the HILL model describes what impactful learning looks like, how should we design assessment in order to serve as a lever for the six other building blocks to really create high impact? Sure, we have seen programmes that include splendid actions to increase urgency for the learners and many options to allow higher learner agency. But in some of these programmes none of these efforts work out since learners only pay attention to one single incentive: getting a sufficient score on the weekly or monthly test.

The 'Assessment as Learning' principles are helpful in designing HILL-proof assessment practices. The Assessment as Learning framework builds further on the

Assessment for Learning approach that has been described in many articles and books by scholars from all over the world (R. Stiggins, M. James, M. Birenbaum, etc.). Therefore, in the next paragraphs, we will integrate the core elements of the Assessment for Learning into the framework of Assessment as Learning.

What is Assessment as Learning about?

In many publications, scholars have defined the characteristics of Assessment for Learning. Assessment for Learning is described as the process of collecting information about the learners' learning process and outcomes from a wide variety of assessment practices; this information is used by the learners to steer, plan and redirect their learning process and by teachers to adapt the support or scaffolds they offer the learner in order to optimally meet the learners' needs (Wiliam, 2011). It implies seeking out, analysing and reflecting on information from students themselves, teachers and the learners' peers as it is expressed in dialogue, learner responses to tasks and questions, and observations. Therefore, assessment is part of everyday learning and teaching in everyday classrooms and workplaces. It happens in real time during the learning process, as an integral aspect of it. It is a part of the learning process and is not separated in an additional test or examination period. It serves primarily as a feedforward moment. It is meant to enhance the learning process, informing the learner how to proceed, and not to judge performance and take high-stake go/no-go decisions (such as not being allowed to participate in another learning programme or course; not being selected for a new role, task or position).

This means that feedback and reflection based upon information collected in real time are the core processes in an Assessment for Learning approach. The primary goal of assessment is enhancing learning itself, with a focus directly on the learner's developing capabilities, while these are in the process of being developed. In the Assessment for Learning framework, the responsibility of the learner in the assessment process is significant. The learner is involved in formulating the learning goals, in planning the learning trajectory, monitoring progress through reflection and feedback, and deciding upon the next steps to take in the learning process. Teachers and peers co-monitor and offer scaffolds in this assessments process. In short, learner agency is central.

More recently, triggered by misinterpretations of the Assessment for Learning framework and fuelled by constructivist learning theories and activity theory for workplace learning (see below), the Assessment for Learning framework has been further developed into the Assessment as Learning framework (Dochy & James, 2017).

In terms of misinterpretations, we refer to the practices of learners taking too many formative tests, and who usually see such tests as being summative. Also, assessment tools of many kinds have been used too much in a sense that they create stress moments, much more so than learning moments or opportunities. A further development in an Assessment as Learning framework will increase impact.

In addition to the aforementioned elements of the Assessment for Learning framework, implementing the Assessment as Learning framework implies:

(1) Contextualising assessment or searching for, collecting and interpreting information on the learning process and outcomes of the learner while he or she is working on a variety of the competences aimed for and relevant tasks. For example, if we aim to ascertain the learner's progress in communicating bad news, a test asking the learner what and how she would communicate in a certain case offers less valid information than observing the learner while he or she is communicating bad news in different contexts. Another example is informing a patient on a diagnosis you derived from information from different sources. Assessment information collected during the learning process indicates what a learner has learned while performing certain tasks.

(2) When learning is social in nature, implying that developing and fine-tuning knowledge, skills and competences asks for relevant others to mirror, to question and to discuss, the community also plays a significant role in supporting learners to assess their progress and to decide on next steps. The learner's community is a more powerful support in an Assessment as Learning approach than external assessors.

(3) Closely related to the former characteristic of Assessment as Learning, the social nature of learning implies that assessment is not only about individual progress in L&D. When learning is a process of collaborative sense-making and developing new insights, assessment of how the group or team dealt with learning is as important as the learning of the individual.

(4) Problem-solving is at the heart of the learning process. Therefore, assessment that informs the learner's learning process addresses how the learner deals with problem-solving tasks.

(5) When learning is about being responsible and self-regulating in using resources or tools (intellectual, human, material) to formulate problems, work productively and evaluate their efforts, assessment that addresses learner agency is informative for the learner.

These five characteristics imply that relevant assessment information can be captured and reported through various forms of recording, including narrative accounts and audio and visual media. The portfolio also has an important role to play here. Moreover, assessment with a more holistic and qualitative character, instead of being solely atomised and quantified as in many measurement approaches, serves the purpose of Assessment as Learning.

James (2012) provides some examples from schools that do practice 3G (third generation) assessments. From such examples and the writings on 3G assessment, we learn that Assessment as Learning should be further developed in the following critical directions for the future:

(1) Authentic assessment based on ongoing performances or 'exit' exhibitions are promoted.

(2) Learners are asked to work across disciplines by creating 'real' learning activities (learner-as-worker).
(3) Learners or instructors both can devise a task, providing they use and understand the principles that underlie its construction. Helping learners to acquire this meta-level understanding is a valued goal.
(4) Learners are challenged to practise using accumulated knowledge and to apply it to new situations.
(5) Learners engage in effective communication in oral, written and graphic forms.
(6) Learners are required to be reflective, persistent and well organised.
(7) A focus on learning is described as the destination for the learners' journey and precise learning objectives are not tightly pre-specified.

Project-based programmes are good examples of how to make Assessment as Learning happen. For example, when learning takes place while executing an authentic project with a client or an external commissioning company, during the project period students receive continuous feedback on how they are progressing through discussion with their teammates and with the client. This immediate feedback is the most important resource to steer the different steps to take in the project. Milestones like project scoping notes and mid-term reports are the input for evaluation, answering the following questions: Where are we heading to (objectives)? How far are we now in executing the project and how are we doing currently? What are the next steps to take? Final reports and other project deliverables are the evidence of the learning outcomes of the team and an important step for reflecting on what has been learned that might fuel future learning and future project teamwork. An additional final test does not offer any additional relevant information for the learner.

Another example that offers opportunities to implement assessment as learning is portfolio assessment. When learners create their own portfolio in order to collect evidence on their learning process and the mastery of several competences, it is the individual reflection on the evidence collected, as well as the feedback dialogue with peers or a coach, that makes the portfolio not only an assessment tool but foremost a powerful learning tool.

In all of these examples, exercising 'agency' in the use of your resources or tools is a key issue in the assessment.

In organisations, PDPs and/or portfolios are widely used to support the employee in the development of competences. This assessment practice offers the opportunity to stimulate the employee in taking responsibility for showing real-time evidence of his or her competences, asking for feedback from relevant others as well as reflecting on the evidence themselves, to plan their L&D trajectory according to their own needs and preferences.

In addition, to a growing extent, work in organisations is organised in teams. These teams offer an important environment to learn from and with each other. At one of the largest petrochemical industries in the Netherlands, we have had the opportunity to support the operational teams and their supervisors to turn the end-of-shift team meeting into a powerful learning and assessment moment. Together with the company, we developed a list of relevant questions to reflect upon with respect to safety behaviour during work. Using these questions as a guide to reflect on as a team and to ask for feedback from team members has proved to be a powerful lever for learning and consequently for working as a team in a safer way.

Why Assessment as Learning?

Our observations in schools and organisations as well as the research results of scholars in many countries have shown the continuing dominance of a test culture in schools and organisations, and its effects.

Overall, many school programmes are overloaded with tests: summative tests, but also so-called formative tests that state 'finally all results of the formative tests will be added up to a final score'. This makes all of these tests summative.

Since too much testing leads to severe disadvantages for many learners, we have to seriously question how many, and what type of, assessments it is wise to take.

Also, and perhaps most importantly, Prof. Wynne Harlen stated clearly a long time ago that, in any programme, too much summative testing squeezes out any form of formative assessment (Harlen & James, 1997).

Given this dominant test-taking culture in our schools, during the past two decades, many researchers, including ourselves, have promoted Assessment for Learning (AfL) as a means to increase learning impact, emphasising the importance of using assessment information, collected during the learning process, for reflection and feedback in order to support the learner in taking the next steps in the learning process. Despite the arguments for reorienting assessment practices towards implementing assessment as a tool for learning, Assessment for Learning has been interpreted in many cases as implementing more 'formative' tests, in some cases ending up with twice as many tests being administered. Both research and practice warn, and sometimes show clear evidence, that formative assessments are seen by students as summative assessments, or are evidently used as partial scores to be added up into

TABLE 3.7

Too much testing leads to...
shallow learning: superficial learning that leads to forgetting quickly afterwards and avoidance of deep-level learning
shadow learning: learners take other extra classes taught by 'shadow teachers'
test training: learners believe that skill in taking tests helps them
stress and demotivation
teaching to the test: instructors tend to focus unconsciously on those issues that will be tested
narrowing down of the programme: as a consequence of the former
increasing the *burden of testing*: learners try to prepare themselves for tests by raising the level of preparation in 'revision classes' and test prep programmes

one final summative score. As a consequence, these are not formative assessments, as claimed, but simply a series of consecutive summative assessments. This turns the experience of learning into a stressful hurdle race. Also, in organisations, assessment mainly has the connotation of taking high-stake decisions.

Assessment – for example, by using assessment centres – is used to decide upon the career of the employee. In training programmes, assessment is organised as end-of-programme tests to decide on certification. Also, performance appraisal interviews are in many cases performance oriented and rarely learning or development oriented. Even when it is communicated that both of the latter purposes are being pursued, employees still often experience the interview as something that is high-stake and adapt their behaviour according to the consequences expected (promotion, salary rise, etc). If the information shared and discussed during performance appraisal interviews is experienced as the main input for promotions and other high-stake decisions, it might be wise not to openly reflect on developmental needs or to choose strategically which developmental needs to place in the picture.

Therefore, for most training programmes, it is wiser not to use the term 'formative assessments', since most of these seem to be in fact summative. Currently, we advise programmes, providers or institutes to speak solely about 'assessments' being summative on the one hand, and 'feedback' on the other hand.

Feedback can be provided in two ways:

(1) Feedback is given by experts or peers continuously when learners are working during meetings, sometimes individually, but mostly in teams. Experts or peers coach the teams by providing feedback during the meetings when moving from team to team. They provide positive feedback, critical questions, suggestions, encouragement, recognition and critical feedback, mostly through open questions, etc.
(2) Feedback can also be provided by peers that are teammates or others. Expansive learning theory would argue that in some cases 'more expert others' or peers could be equally effective. Research shows that feedback by peers can be as valuable as that given by experts depending upon the content and situation. A learning climate in which peers provide positive feedback and question our work can be stimulating for any learner, provided that it is given in a constructive spirit.

Constructive feedback always gives learners the incentive to acquire expertise

A last remark I want to make here about Assessment as Learning concerns our habits of giving feedback. Most of us tend to see feedback as signalling what can be done better. We learn a lot from mistakes, but a safe climate is needed for us to explore reasons for our mistakes and ways of doing things better. In order to keep learners motivated, and to strive for a learning climate that is safe, providing constructive feedback is a condition *sine qua non.*

I recommend that coaches provide feedback in a way that the learner always receives a majority of constructive task-oriented feedback over negative task-feedback. This is much harder to do than it might sound. Certainly, for less talented learners in a specific area, finding positive remarks and encouragement might be a hard task. Imagine one of your most problematic learners who did not master a specific issue really quickly. Although you might have thought that he was probably stupid, try to imagine what type of constructive feedback you could give to such a person:

- Your introduction was well written!
- The structure of your report was clear!
- The layout of the piece was really attractive!
- I read some bright ideas!
- I did like the variation in figures that you used as illustrations!
  And…
- Nevertheless, I think you could better question your problem solution again. Are you convinced it is correct? Why?
- And I am not sure whether your summary reflects the key issues of your argumentation. Do you think this can be done better?

Always providing some constructive feedback, i.e. identifying strengths before highlighting weaknesses, gives learners the incentive to continue on the road to acquiring expertise.

If a dominant test culture is not the way to go, what then is the direction we should be heading in?

Some years ago, I went horseback riding on the moors just outside Exeter, UK, with Professor Mary James. Mary is a world expert on assessment. When galloping through Dartmoor National Park, we had an exciting talk about the future of assessment. As you can guess, the immediate result was that I kept on thinking about assessment in the future. More concretely, an immediate result was that, on Mary's recommendation (formative feedback), I put rubber mats on the floors of my horse stables in order to save hours of daily cleaning. In the mid-term I kept on playing with the idea of 'developmental assessment' that I had discussed with Mary James.

Assessment as Learning builds upon constructivist theories and activity theories of learning by scholars from both Europe and the US: linguists such as Noam Chomsky, computer scientists such as Herbert Simon, and cognitive scientists such as Jerome Bruner (who in his later writings moved towards socio-cultural activity theories; see Bruner, 1996). More recently, neuroscientists have joined these ranks (James, 2006).

Just a few words on the core message of these theories on learning as a stepping stone towards the foundations of the Assessment as Learning approach.

Constructivist theories argue that learning requires the active engagement of learners. The focus is on how learners cognitively construct meaning by organising structures, concepts and principles in individual (when learning individually) or team mental models or shared mental models (when learning as a team) (Decuyper et al., 2010). Prior knowledge here is seen as a springboard for future learning and a powerful determinant of learning (Robert Glaser in Dochy, 1992). Problem-solving is used as an environment for knowledge construction, using processing strategies, and to organise knowledge in expert structures. Monitoring, regulating and controlling the learner's own learning during the different phases of task execution (from planning to action to evaluation), cognitively, motivationally and emotionally, are the self-regulatory processes needed to develop the competences aimed for and to travel the road towards professional expertise.

Activity theories of learning go back to Dewey and Russian psychologists such as Leontiev and Vygotsky, who describe human development and learning as a transaction between the individual and the environment. These scholars have certainly influenced more recent scholars such as Bruner and Engeström. The latter is known principally for reconfiguring Russian activity theory as an explanation of how learning happens in the workplace.

In activity theory, learning is by definition a collaborative activity in which learners develop their thinking together. Working in groups, teamwork of cooperative learning is not a choice, since learning involves cooperation and what is learned is not necessarily the property of an individual but shared within the social group, hence the concept of 'distributed or shared cognition' (James, 2006).

Constructivist theory has had a large influence on practices of learning and instruction, with many schools as well as L&D programmes implementing problem-based learning approaches, project learning, case-based learning, and so on. The more advanced activity theory, or as I earlier called it, the 'expansive learning theory' or the 'theory of inter-organisational learning' (Dochy, Gijbels, Segers, & Van den Bossche, 2010), has not yet had such a strong translation into learning and instruction practices.

We agree with Mary James that such a theory implies that the instructor needs to create an environment in which learners can be stimulated to think and act in authentic tasks (like apprentices) beyond their current level of competence (but in what Vygotsky calls their zone of proximal development). James was one of the first scientists who tried to bring what is called '3G learning theory' into practice (James, 2006).

3G learning theory

From this third generation (3G) theoretical point of view, accessing and using appropriate tools is key to expansive learning. Appropriateness of tools means the following: It is important to support activities that a learner can complete while coached by others but not alone so that the 'more expert other', in some cases an instructor but often a peer, can 'scaffold' the learning. According to James (2012),

tasks need to be collaborative and learners need to be involved both in the generation of problems and of solutions. Learners and coaches jointly solve problems and
everyone develops their competences.

Framing assessment from an activity theoretical point of view only started
very recently and builds further upon the framework of Assessment for Learning,
described above. As James argued, learning can result from active participation in
authentic (real-world) activities or projects. What does 3G assessment look like?
According to James (2006):

> the focus here is on how well people exercise 'agency' in their use of the
> resources or tools (intellectual, human, material) available to them to formu-
> late problems, work productively and evaluate their efforts. Learning out-
> comes can be captured and reported through various forms of recording,
> including audio- and visual media.
>
> *(James, 2006, p. 58)*

Within this frame, portfolios can be interesting tools, and when building learning identities is central to learning then certainly students' own self-assessments
must be central. This is strongly supported by John Hattie's famous research on
what elements do really affect learning and education: he found only one element
to have a tremendous impact on learning, with an effect size over 1.4, and that is
the use of self-report grades.

Likewise, what we called 'Assessment as Learning' advocates the use of data that
are collected during the learning process as information to evaluate the learning.
Well-known examples are project outcomes or products and portfolios (see also our
earlier work *Alternatives in Assessment* (Birenbaum & Dochy, 1996) and *Optimizing
New Modes of Assessment* (Segers, Dochy, & Cascallar, 2003)).

*3G assessment does not necessarily intertwine with IT or computerised assessment.
Actually, mostly it doesn't at all.*

James tried further to operationalise 3G assessment with the following pointers
styled 'third generation assessment':

*   If learning cannot be separated from the actions in which it is embodied, then
    assessment too must be 'situated'.
*   Assessment alongside learning implies that it needs to be done by the com-
    munity rather than by external assessors.
*   Assessment of group learning is as important as the learning of the individual.
*   'In vivo' studies of complex problem-solving may be the most appropriate
    form for assessments to take.

- The focus should be on how well people exercise 'agency' in their use of the resources or tools (intellectual, human, material) to formulate problems, work productively and evaluate their efforts.
- Learning outcomes can be captured and reported through various forms of recording, including narrative accounts and audio and visual media.
- Evaluation needs to be more holistic and qualitative, not atomised and quanti-fied as in measurement approaches.

(James, 2012, p. 195)

Empirical evidence on the impact of Assessment as Learning

In school settings, our own studies have been building further on the early work of researchers such as Black and Wiliam (1998) and Kingston and Nash (2011).

The studies of Baas (2017) and colleagues showed that implementing Assessment for Learning in primary school practices predicts students' strategy use. Specifically, the results reveal that monitoring activities that inform students on their progress and their strengths and weaknesses predict students' strategy use in the forethought phase. Students engage more in task orientation and planning activities. Promoting student learning by providing scaffolds that aid students in taking the next step in their learning predicts students' strategy use during the phases of task execu-tion and self-reflection. Assessment for Learning practices positively predict the use of surface learning strategies, deep-level learning strategies and process evaluation. While it is generally assumed that the use of deep-level learning strategies results in higher-quality learning than the use of surface learning strategies, the enhanced use of both deep-level and surface learning strategies is a first step for young students towards developing their repertoire of learning strategies and coming to understand when to apply certain learning strategies. In sum, the findings underpin the notion that Assessment for Learning is a powerful tool to enhance students' cognitive and meta-cognitive strategy use.

The studies of Pat-El (2012) and colleagues addressed students' as well as teach-ers' perceptions of the extent to which Assessment for Learning is implemented in secondary schools. The results show that students' and teachers' perceptions of the level to which Assessment for Learning is practised in classrooms are largely incongruent. Teachers perceive far more practice of Assessment for Learning than students. Moreover, these incongruencies have a strong negative impact on stu-dents' motivation. In classrooms where there is a congruence between teachers and students in how they experience Assessment as Learning being present, stu-dents show more feelings of personal competence and autonomy to learn in their own way.

The studies of Gabelica et al. (2012) addressed Assessment for Learning practices at the team level. In a series of experimental studies with university students, they underpinned the importance of team feedback and reflexivity for enhancing team performance.

Beausaert (2012) and his co-researchers conducted a systematic literature review which yielded inconclusive results concerning the relation between the use of PDPs by employees and engaging in learning activities. Inspired by these results, they conducted a survey study. The results of Beausaert's study on the use of PDPs by pharmacy assistants showed differentiated results. It was found that users of a PDP undertook more learning activities (in the past) than non-users. However, pharmacy assistants who used a PDP did not plan more learning activities. They did not plan to undertake further training more often than non-PDP users. This finding might indicate that PDPs are especially used as feedback tools and not as feedforward tools. In other words, it is expected that the tools are often used for looking back, to discuss learning activities that have been undertaken. They do not serve as a tool to look forward and to support employees in the planning of future learning activities.

Follow-up studies indicated that although PDPs are valid tools for performance appraisal, their power lies in supporting employees in their professional development. More concretely, the results of the studies indicate that the use of a PDP stimulates employees to reflect on the extent to which they possess the competences necessary for their job and on the learning activities undertaken to enhance the level of proficiency of the job competences. Furthermore, PDPs lead to a diagnosis of the gaps in job competences and stimulates employees to plan further learning activities.

These results imply that in order to make employees undertake learning activities and improve their performance by using a PDP, introducing and using the PDP as a tool for L&D is the most effective method. Finally, Beausaert and his colleagues investigated whether the level of implementation of a PDP influences its effects. The results of their study revealed that if the employee reflects on the PDP and learns from it and if the supervisor is perceived as motivating, the employee is far more likely to undertake more learning activities, show more expertise-growth and flexibility towards changing circumstances, and perform better. In sum, reasons for the effectiveness of the PDP as an 'Assessment as Learning' tool can be found in the way the assessment process is set up and organised and/or in the presence of various supporting process conditions (learning and reflection and a motivating supervisor).

Note

1 www.maastrichtuniversity.nl/education/why-um/problem-based-learning

4

THE HILL MODEL IN PRACTICE

Tips and guidelines

After an analysis of your training programme (see Chapter 6: Applications of HILL), you can decide to work with your team to increase the impact of your programme through focusing on one or more of the HILL building blocks that are still not fully developed or are lacking, or otherwise focus on one or more of the HILL building blocks that you want to strengthen as the core profile of your learning programme or module.

I recently visited an organisation that did strengthen all of the modules of its core Learning and Development (L&D) programme, based on three HILL building blocks: increasing the hybridity of all modules, implementing collaborative learning, and intensive coaching in the modules; and by focusing on more action and knowledge sharing throughout the courses. In many of these modules, trainers planned clear sequences of online work and face-to-face meetings to increase hybridity; the face-to-face meetings largely consisted of authentic work in small teams with a high level of interaction and many occasions and events (also online) to share information within and across the teams. It looked like a small revolution for the learners, trainers and the organisation, and experiences with the new modules led to a lot of enthusiasm and strong satisfaction.

From the background information in Chapter 4, we can derive several concrete guidelines for strengthening each specific HILL building block. Based upon the research findings we analysed and summarised as well as our own experiences in many programmes, in this chapter we provide you with some support in translating the building blocks into real actions. This is not to say that the tips below are exhaustive; instead, they should serve as a source of inspiration for you to check what actions fit your organisation, or to come to other actions that are better suited to the culture of your teams.

Of course, creating impact will be largely facilitated by the context and the learning climate in the organisation. For example, having a shared vision on learning, the programme and the organisational strategy will surely foster the impact. Such a shared vision should be short, consist of no more than three clear issues, can be expressed in one sentence, should be composed through many iterations of interaction between the different organisational levels, should then be repeated and spread over and over again in the organisation, and finally should be a core message in the organisation's learner marketing.

In our own research, we have seen (when analysing organisations' shared vision) too many organisations without a vision, or without a shared vision. I still remember our interviewers coming back from several organisations where the director or CEO told a nice cohesive story, meant to be the organisation's general vision, but which did not coincide in any way with what was written on their website. Or even worse, CEOs would give an explanation of the organisation's vision which later on seemed to be contradictory to what their website said. Also, some managers tried to sell us their 'shared vision', while employees admitted they had never heard about it or admitted that they know that 'such things are always top-down here'.

According to Senge (1990), having a shared vision and people that master 'systems thinking' are key requirements for an organisation to learn. Systems thinking means looking at the organisation from a distance, considering different perspectives and how these influence each other in order to understand the patterns beyond the problems faced. It helps you not to draw on quick and dirty solutions to daily problems. Systems thinking helps to define the L&D agenda in the long term, with a portfolio of learning activities that aim to deal with upcoming challenges in a sustainable way. Also, bringing the learning close to work, to authentic situations and to the real problem of the organisation that learners themselves can 'feel' definitely will enhance impact.

A change in mindset and way of acting will mostly be stimulated when we change our jargon. We recommend that organisations, training institutes, programmes, etc. stop using classroom language such as 'teachers', lessons, or teaching', but to create a whole new vocabulary that clearly expresses the target of creating impact, such as knowledge creation labs, change labs, transformational labs, coaches, work sessions, just-in-time expert lectures, just-in-time webinars, HILL sessions, discussion meetings, wrap-up sessions, knowledge sharing meetings, basic knowledge training programmes, act and perform sessions, pitch and present meetings.

Before we present some tips and guidelines, we would like to stress that the HILL model is based on research that has mostly been conducted in Western countries, meaning that some of the building blocks will not have a straightforward fit with Asian, African or South American cultures. This implies that for non-Western organisations, as well as for organisations working with employees from non-Western backgrounds, a careful reflection on how the proposed building blocks are experienced by their employees is necessary.

Urgency, gap, problem

This first building block can be described as a clearly argued problem, a challenge, gap or problem experienced that creates a sense of urgency for an individual or a group. This sense of urgency is an ideal starting point for a learning process.

While the other building blocks of the HILL model concern the learning process itself, we start off by asking ourselves where it all starts. Why would anyone learn something? What can – or should – be the starting point of a learning process that results in – or rather induces – HILL?

Any learning process that aims to strengthen the potential for HILL, in our opinion, has to start from a clearly substantiated problem, an experienced challenge, or an item that creates a certain sense of *urgency*. Such a sense of urgency can originate from an explicit experience that a certain problem needs to be solved urgently, from strong argumentation, from the power of persuasion from a problem owner, or from a feeling of strong interest in a certain phenomenon.

Triggers such as these push a learner to step into a learning situation with maximal commitment and intrinsic motivation. This 'state of flow' (Csikszentmihalyi & Beattie, 1979) arises when there is an optimal balance between the task requirements for the learner, and his/her previously acquired competences. When the task is a routine task or frequently occurring problem, the potential for a state of flow to be established will be low. Such a routine problem can probably be solved on autopilot. For the learner, it would be a quick fix, and he or she would move on to the next issue. There would be no reason to reach High Impact Learning. However, the case where the level of competence of the learner is highly insufficient to tackle the problem or challenge is also not a rich environment that would stimulate commitment and intrinsic motivation within the learner. In other words: when a supervisor aims to stimulate an employee to invest in learning, he or she has to take into account this balance. When new roles or tasks need to be taken up, it is the responsibility of the supervisor to carefully consider which employees might be suitable, given their current competence profile, and what support they need to further develop the competences needed.

From theories on motivation, interest and learning processes, we know that motivation and interest are strong drivers for efficient learning processes. Interest and motivation can be seen as necessary but insufficient conditions to lead to impact. They are *insufficient* because learning progress is influenced by a combination of the learner, the coaching, and other contextual factors. They are *necessary* because without motivation, a learning process wouldn't last or even start. Reading things just-in-time, being able to immediately spot the added value of the things you learned, having the opportunity to frequently apply what you learned in a project or daily activities, etc. are necessary triggers that spur on the learner. Starting from an mismatch between the learner's competences and the expectations or requirements of a task creates a sense of urgency that can motivate the learner to go the extra mile and invest more energy in his/her own learning or developmental process.

Getting the chance to express your expectations and to make your own interests or dreams concrete, and having the possibility to try to fulfil your interests or to pursue your dreams within a learning programme gives you the ultimate drive to go all the way.

I remember meeting by accident a group of my own students in a café in Leuven late at night, all of them highly involved in a hot discussion. When I enquired what they were discussing, they frankly replied 'the company's problem that we ran into in our project', referring to the learning project that we had discussed that day. It seemed that their enthusiasm and involvement had become so enhanced that they even discussed the issues in their free time. What more could I wish for? In the next meeting, they came up with several alternative problem solutions to study further.

In short, problems, challenges or gaps are the triggers for an employee to participate in an L&D programme. Urgency is the motivational lever for the learner to fully take advantage of the other building blocks, creating a powerful learning environment. Therefore, problems, challenges and gaps that the employee experiences should be the basis of each training activity.

How to create urgency?

Working with problems, cases or projects are well-known methods to increase the authenticity and attractiveness of a learning situation, which often results in a greater sense of learning that can in turn lead to experiencing learning as something pleasant.

Stimulating or creating a sense of urgency at all levels of training is highly complicated. Earlier, we argued that a clear experience, strong argumentation, or the power of persuasion from the problem owner can contribute to this sense of urgency, but a strong interest in a phenomenon can already suffice. Sometimes, working in teams and formulating shared goals can clarify the urgency to the learner(s). Also, making sure that the problem owner is close at hand increases urgency (either the learner herself is the problem owner – she wants to solve a specific problem, or a client's problem; or she can choose his own interest as a starting base for tackling a problem; or otherwise the problem owner is cooperating in the learning project).

We have organised the tips to create urgency into seven groups: fuelling curiosity and energy; an authentic problem as a trigger; closing the gap; setting goals; facilitate; make relevance of investing in learning explicit; and experience and feedback.

Fuelling curiosity and energy

- Curiosity empowers a person to learn; it is the basis of learning: fuel the learner's curiosity by triggering why-questions, by being curious yourself as a coach. If you are not a curious person, you are not a learner (David Fox, 2017).
- Answer a question with questions; do not immediately play the expert that knows all of the answers – it might kill curiosity.
- Start off as a trainer with energy and transfer this energy to the learners.
- Make learning an energising activity; energy helps to create flow.
- Start from the personal interests of learners or at least connect to them.

An authentic problem as a trigger

- Start from a problem; one that is as authentic as possible: take time to brainstorm and discuss the problem with the learner in order to trigger curiosity to understand and solve the problem; to create ownership.
- Make the authenticity of the problem explicit from the start of the learning journey, for example by inviting a third party (client, organisation, stakeholder, club etc) to formulate and describe the project assignment.
- Use highly current problems or challenges they will face in the future and that have been on the agenda in team meetings.
- Embed the problem in a real-life case.
- Organise an immersion day: immerse learners into real cases.
- Take time to brainstorm, to create mindmaps, to unravel a problem or a client's initial question.
- Work with authentic material, real information from the professional field, instead of information adapted or designed for training purposes.
- Go outside: look around and visit reality.
- Involve the problem owner, he or she is the one that is confronted with the problem daily.
- Invite speakers/experts that have tackled comparable problems.
- Let the learner/employee figure out how the problem could be solved, and facilitate the search process (without giving away the solution).

Closing the gap

- Let employees themselves reflect on competences or knowledge and skills needed, for example by involving employees in strategic discussions on the future of the organisation or unit. This helps the employee to foresee the new roles and tasks to be fulfilled in the future and opens the discussion about what is needed in terms of competences. This analysis of competences needed is the stepping stone towards collaboratively defining the gaps in competences and the support needed to close the gap. Invest time in letting the employee explain how he or she perceives the gap.

Setting goals

- Ask learners to think about the questions 'where am I now?' and 'where do I have to go to?' Coach the learner towards formulating his or her own learning question(s); this is intensive, but it pays back.
- Let learners describe what is challenging for them.
- Ask the learner to make his or her burning ambition explicit.
- Formulate goals both at the individual and team level: what are we aiming at, what is on the horizon we want to reach? Ask learners to describe their ambitions, what their interest is, what their future plans are. Let them describe their own goals, and to discuss and state their individual and team goals.

- When you set goals, take into account that learners are not blank slates. They have a lot of very relevant experiences and in many cases a rich knowledge and skills base. Let learners bring up this richness of experiences and prior knowledge; leave space and time for doing this and use it as a lever for formulating goals in terms of the next steps in their L&D process.
- Expectation management: check and discuss the expectations of the learners at the start and during a learning trajectory.

Facilitate

- Negotiate on more time and space for the learner's own development; make it part of the organisation's brand box.
- Avoid an assessment system or a set of tests that kill 'personal urgency'.
- Make sure the learner has a complete picture of the whole process, if bits and pieces of this have to be learned; seeing and knowing the end-product is crucial.

Make the relevance of investing in learning explicit

- Discuss why an organisation invests so much in this learning trajectory.
- Demonstrate an increase in efficiency that learners will be able to reach when they master the content/method/application.
- Provide arguments that show that learners can speed up their career progression.
- Provide evidence that what will be learned is key to what will be needed or done.
- Let learners ask themselves: What's in it for me? And use this as a starting point.
- Perform a needs assessment with the learners.
- Use a 360-degree feedback report as a starting point.

Experience and feedback

- When eventually needed, give learners a 'practice shock' – let them perform in practice even if you know they will fail in order to learn from failures.
- Use feedback of supervisors, managers or clients.
- Fuel the feeling of urgency through regular feedback dialogue with the learners.
- Discuss mistakes, incorrect solutions; analyse the process and discuss the approach.

Learner agency

This second building block, learner agency, focuses on ownership of the learner over his/her own learning. Every professional or individual is a manager: a manager of his/her own thinking, acting and functioning. Learner agency originates when a learner takes learning into his/her own hands. As such, learner agency is a *mindset or attitude* to adopt and to develop: day after day, the learner chooses to take up responsibility and ownership for his/her own learning and professional conduct. From this view, learning should not be regarded as something that is 'achieved' after following an L&D programme or educational programme. Instead, learning is something you need to keep thinking of and working on every day of your professional and personal life.

Learner agency enables a learner to (keep on) grow(ing). Not only within his/ her organisation, job or function, but also in general functioning. It's those people who take their lives into their own hands that achieve what no one thought possible. Steve Jobs, for example, wanted in his companies Apple or NeXT only creative employees that were willing to take on challenges, with a learner mindset.

A strong reflective attitude is an inseparable part of a self-managing learner that takes up agency. Reflection is the ability to explicitly look back on and think about your own actions (Schön, 1983). One can reflect on two general moments: after action, or in action. Reflection-on-action takes place after the actual action: after completion, you look back on how you did, how it went etc. Reflection-in-action occurs when you actively reflect while acting, which makes it possible to make adjustments on the way. Both reflection-on-action and reflection-in-action are important, but the latter is harder to accomplish. It requires a higher level of self-awareness and ownership. Professional activities contain dynamic, complex and diverse social interactions that have a significant impact on our functioning. It is important to keep an eye on these components, so that you can adjust when things go wrong. This holds for a trainer, but also for the structural engineer who has to take into account the client's wishes and expectations, the possibilities of his team and the building site, and the town planning determined by the city. The consequence of this multiplicity of factors to take into account is that hardly anything ever goes as you planned it. Being flexible, and being able to reflect, will enable you to make adjustments: as a professional or a learner, you can adjust your own actions (or vision, attitude), you can stimulate your environment to start acting differently, and you see (other) opportunities to reach your goals.

The flexibility to deal with unexpected problems, the guts to try a different approach, and the openness to alternatives make learner agency a strong pillar of High Impact Learning.

How to create learner agency?

A High Impact Learning environment allows for a high amount of 'learner agency': it is not a trainer, an LMS or a teacher that determines and structures everything beforehand; instead, it is the learner him- or herself that has an increasing influence on what he/she does and learns, and how. The learner crafts his/her own L&D trajectory. Agency emerges when the learner takes the next move: he or she takes initiative, acts on and decides on his/her learning process. Agency implies that learners are able to estimate the consequences of their choices, and accept these consequences.

In other words, agency is taking up responsibility for your own choices, the actions you perform, and the consequences for yourself and your environment. We have organised the tips to create learner agency into four groups: goal setting; openness to alternatives; support; and room for own choices.

Goal setting

- Let learners formulate individual and/or team goals.
- Halfway through the programme, make learners rethink their own learning goals and adapt these.

Openness to alternatives

- Allow flexibility in (pathways to) solutions.
- Stimulate finding original paths to solutions.

Support

- Make use of a PDP (personal development plan) or LDP (leadership development plan).
- Providing an oversupply of training programmes in a catalogue does not enhance learner agency.
- Use mid-period reviews as a coaching moment.
- Allow room for and stimulate reflection (How did we do? Was it efficient? Can we do this better/differently? Why? How will we do this next time?).
- Give adequate feedback, both on a task-level and on a process-level.
- Next to critical feedback, also provide constructive feedback.
- Always provide more constructive feedback compared to critique.
- Trust the learner.
- Make sure you know the learner: remember his/her name to start with.
- Build a culture where failing and making mistakes is allowed. Start with yourself: show that you recognise your mistakes, and demonstrate how you learn from them.
- Lead by example – share 'failure stories' – manage reactions to others' mistakes.
- Use a portfolio as a tool for guidance.
- Make sure you build a learning culture: It's okay to make mistakes and learn from them.
- Provide learners ways to excel in electives (e.g. different levels).
- Organise opportunities for learners to present their achievements to peers.
- Provide variation to choose from in online learning paths (video, instruction, text, assignment, or any other path).
- Provide more open course programmes.
- Integrate virtual action learning (VAL).
- Think how you can make the learners the owners of what they will do/learn; discuss this with them.

- Let the learner produce their own product.
- Open schooling: let learners choose and prove their competence through argumentation and documentation instead of organising pass/fail tests. This provides space to take ownership, while traditional testing usually hinders ownership.
- Give employees 'training and development' opportunities instead of a financial end-of-year bonus.
- Use flipped classrooms that learners can plan as they want and have face-to-face meetings at prescheduled times.

Room for own choices

- Give learners opportunities to choose to develop their own talents, interests, and so on.
- Give learners the responsibility to manage their own project.
- Let learners select their own peer learners that join their project team.
- Let learners choose goals.
- Give voice and choice!
- Gradually allow for more choices, and ask learners to respect the consequences of their choice(s).
- Learner agency is about the choices one has within a learning programme: give learners the room to determine which learning activities and approaches to undertake, multiple pathways to follow.

Collaboration and coaching

There is substantial scientific evidence that collaborative learning is effective and therefore should be central in learning programmes. There are many different forms of collaborative learning, in which it is taking place in a variety of ways such as cooperative learning, case-based learning, project-based learning, problem-based learning, buddy systems, etc. Variation is crucial in learning, so we believe that diverse collaborative forms of working and learning should comprise at least one-third of the programme and not exceed two-thirds.

How to create collaboration?

We have organised the tips to create collaboration into two groups: implement collaborative learning; and support learning through collaboration.

Implement collaborative learning

- Implement teamwork as an opportunity for employees to learn from each other.
- When the work is not organised in teams, facilitate and stimulate small-group work to deal with certain questions or tasks. It creates an opportunity to learn

from colleagues. Implement different types of working in small groups, from dyads, triads to teams with up to seven team members.

- Organise a world café.
- Use a speed dating session to introduce learners to each other.
- Organise the work into projects.
- Projects for external clients increase the stake of the outcome to be delivered and therefore stimulate making optimal use of the expertise of all team members.
- Use (interprofessional) communities of practice.
- Organise workplace learning in interprofessional teams.
- Let learners choose buddies.
- Integrate Facebook groups and discussion forums in the process.
- Implement workplace learning and internships in dyads.
- Create enough variation in collaborative methods used.

Support learning through collaboration

- Use coaching at the right time to turn the collaboration into a learning opportunity.
- Try to create open, clear and honest communication.
- Try to create dialogue.
- 'Just-in-time' reflection and intervision about the professional products being created.
- Give constructive feedback.
- Listen and do not judge. Again: when asked, give constructive feedback.
- Increase motivation by allocating increasing responsibilities.

How to implement coaching?

There are many types of coaching. Here, we focus on individual coaching for a safe climate, and team coaching. According to Barendsen and Dochy (2017), team coaching contributes to team effectiveness and team innovativeness. It can also overcome well-known pitfalls and increase perceived efficiency and improve the team climate. Team coaching can have an increased impact on the level of change and development within organisations due to its systemic approach, but the group dynamics, the developmental level of the team and the team's commitment during the coaching process certainly also play an important role. A crucial aspect of coaching is the feedback dialogue between the learner and the coach. Therefore, in addition to tips for a safe climate and tips to coach a team, we formulate some tips for the feedback dialogue.

Tips to coach for a safe climate

- Coaches know all learners by name.
- Coaches speak out about the talents of learners and their trust in their high quality.

- Coaches speak out about individual qualities and rewards.
- Model that you are a curious, excited person about learning; that you are curious about learning new things (David Fox, 2017).
- Set up learning environments where people see how much reward there is in being a curious person (David Fox, 2017).
- Set high expectations.

Tips to coach a team

- Stimulate team communication.
- Provide feedback on occurring team interaction processes.
- Support the team to enhance the quality of their interactions.
- Create an open and trusting atmosphere and where learners feel safe to share ideas and learn from each other.
- Focus on building shared commitment.
- Set clear expectations concerning team outputs.
- Encourage collaborative efforts.
- Stimulate team consensus on procedures and team goals.
- Provide encouragement and feedback.
- Provide insight into the team's way of working and identify areas of improvement.
- Encourage desirable performance behaviours.
- Give recognition and celebrate small successes.
- Intensify interpersonal relationships.
- Address conflicts openly and equip team members with conflict management skills for the future.
- Empower members by delegating tasks.
- Steer towards dividing responsibilities among team members.
- Encourage team members to give others the opportunity to experiment and work out problems on their own, instead of immediately providing solutions.
- Stimulate and encourage teams to coach themselves.
- Preferably, your coaching should be voluntary where both coach and coachee perceive mutual benefits of engaging in the coaching process.
- Stop, look back, think and plan forward.
- Help the learners to think about a coordinated and task-appropriate use of their collective resources.
- Monitor and scaffold not only the cognitive process of dealing with the task, but also the process of dealing with group processes.
- Stimulate and challenge learners to critically question their thinking in order to further extend, modify or deepen their understanding.
- Stimulate team members to act as a team.
- Stimulate a shared commitment to the team and its task.
- Stimulate the team to critically reflect on the alignment of strategies and procedures used.

- Monitor and stimulate the contribution of each team member in order to make optimal use of the different expertise available.
- Stimulate team members to critically question and debate each other's contributions.
- Make sure that team members feel that it is safe to speak up, to not agree, and to discuss divergent ideas. Take actions to increase feelings of safety, e.g. spending some time on informal activities so that members get to know each other from another perspective.
- Ask your team members after a few weeks to reflect individually on the golden principles for successful team collaboration (that they come up with themselves). To what extent is the team working according to these 'principles'? Are all principles relevant? What critical events happened that might have caused negative tensions in the team? How did you deal with it as a team? What positive flow did you experience as a team? What evoked this? To what extent do you feel that your team reflected on the team cooperation during the project work? Discuss this in the team. And decide eventually to reformulate the golden principles.
- Focus on the strengths of peers.
- Dialogue on outcomes.
- Support reflection and self-evaluation.
- Dialogue for inquiry and feedback.
- Give the feedback a developmental and not an evaluative purpose.
- Remember 'situated coaching': coaching behaviours can be more or less suitable depending on the team context and progression of the team.

'But where do we get the time for a feedback dialogue?'

- Implement a system of peer feedback.
- Organise the feedback dialogue on the group level, focusing on patterns observed in the work done and stimulating peers to learn from each other.
- Individual feedback dialogue is just walking and talking – during meetings, learners should work constantly; coaches should '*walk and talk*' (= constantly questioning, engaging, motivating, challenging = providing feedback).
- Ask for self-study beforehand, so that your hours of contact time can focus on 'digging deeper', on action.
- Plan your feedback dialogue; use a system such as e.g. Feedpulse.
- View feedback dialogue as a part of the learning process.
- Put the responsibility on the learners.
- Make a more strict selection of relevant goals to aim for; aim for quality in learning instead of quantity. Less content gives more time for feedback.

Hybrid learning

All learning is a mix of different methods and formats nowadays, so all learning is blended. With this building block, we stress the importance of hybrid learning to

TABLE 4.1

'Online'	'Offline'
• video or web conferencing and chats • searching information on the internet • using YouTube	• face-to-face work meetings • studying materials on your own

create impact, **a well-thought-out mix between online and offline learning**. In short, this is a sequence of activities that follows an 'online/face-to-face, online/face-to-face, online/face-to-face, online/face-to-face etc' sequence with well-thought-out frequency and duration adapted to the context, domain, level of learners, etc.

How to enhance hybrid learning?

We have organised the tips to enhance hybridity in two categories: tips to design hybridity and tips to support hybrid learning.

Design

- Create hybridity in learning modules, a sequence of activities that follow an 'online/face-to-face, online/face-to-face, online/face-to-face, online/face-to-face etc' sequence with well-thought-out frequency and duration.
- Think about alternative ways of hybrid learning such as the use of discussion forums, the use of social media, etc., in addition to the traditional way of making learning objects available online.
- Always start hybrid learning trajectories with a face-to-face meeting.
- Invest in time for someone to keep the discussion board going.
- 'Variation is the key of learning' (Marton, 1999).
- Vary face-to-face activities: discussion, interaction, collaborative work, presenting, inspiration sessions, storytelling sessions etc.
- Keep on alternating online learning (chatrooms, videos, shared work on assignments, e-content, webinars, games etc), and offline learning (face-to-face sharing, discussion, just-in-time lectures, mini-panels, etc.).

Support

- Stimulate learners to create and post their own YouTube video based on your assignments.
- Stimulate interaction and collaboration among learners, online as well as offline.
- Stimulate reflection as a useful step in defining the next steps in the learning trajectory.

- Support learners in making argued choices on how to go through the online learning offers, to craft their own learning trajectory.
- Make explicit to the learner the purpose of the offline and online activities and why the hybridity is designed as it is.
- Ask for feedback from the learners about the hybridity.
- Check the learners' computer self-efficacy. If it is low, support the learner in getting to know how to use the online learning opportunities and to develop confidence in his or her online learning abilities.

Action and knowledge sharing

In training, workplace learning and classes, learners cannot be active enough. Learners should most of the time be busy exploring, experimenting, testing, (re-) formulating hypotheses, evaluating hypotheses, making errors and learning from them, planning, reflecting and monitoring (Michael, 2006). Active learning and knowledge sharing should go hand in hand: learning should become a process of linking practice to concepts through different iterations that is created and further deepened through discussions and/or collaboration.

Organisations could use their L&D programme to tailor their strategic policy to their employees. Sharing is a key in a good, acceptable and powerful translation.

How to enhance action and knowledge sharing?

We have formulated tips on how to realise an infrastructure for action and knowledge sharing and how to support and facilitate learners.

Infrastructure for action and knowledge sharing

- Practice 'learning by doing' by implementing debriefing sessions, time-out sessions during work, to briefly reflect on the work done and check whether improvements are needed.
- Implement a variety of active learning methods: problem-based learning, case-based learning, cooperative/collaborative learning/teamwork; think-pair-share or peer instruction; inquiry-based learning; discovery learning; and technology-enhanced learning, etc.
- Increase diversity (in age and expertise, background) in teams according to the differences in expertise needed to get the work done.
- Coach diversity in order to make it an asset: start with individual reflections, follow up with 'small-group discussions' and end with 'whole group agreement' (Rosseel, 2017).
- In a face-to-face setting, use round tables; don't work as a teacher in front of a class.
- If your training or programme runs with multiple teams of learners, try to align your working rooms and facilities with HILL: permanent working rooms for teams and communities.

- Create a workbox series (share and document best evidence).
- Ask learners to share best evidence or cases on the learning platform.
- Encourage snack learning by sharing: share daily your event.
- Connect communities to practice.
- Do people talk to each other?
- Use smaller working rooms for teams that can be reserved for teamwork only.
- Implement intervision meetings.
- Provide a platform to exchange experiences and information.

Facilitate and support

- Stimulate peer discussion and interaction in teams.
- Stimulate sharing information in all possible ways (face-to-face, platforms, apps, etc.) by leading by example (walk the talk).
- When using an LMS, it should strongly support the sharing of know-how, of work in progress and of products between learners and learner and coaches. (Blackboard and clones of blackboard are usually weak in this).
- Encourage a climate of respect for each other's findings/input.

Flexibility – formal and informal learning

As learners, we can learn in classrooms, but we learn many things outside of formally structured and planned situations. We learn at work from problems, from errors, from questions, from changes, critical incidents, challenges, etc. in the authentic situation itself and this sometimes adds to future performance improvement. More informal learning can only be enhanced through installing as much and as well as possible the optimal conditions for informal learning to appear. If learners never meet each other, chances for informal learning will decrease. If learners work together in the same room for a considerable amount of time during a week, informal learning is highly likely to appear. Although the 70/20/10 model does not have any scientific grounding, the application of it in many organisations has already stimulated the use of workplace learning and sometimes of informal learning as well.

How to enhance flexibility?

Facilitate

- Dare to deviate from the training manual to open up room for the learner to craft his or her own learning path.
- Leave room in the training programme for casual learning moments.
- Discuss mistakes as powerful opportunities for learning.
- Use discussion moments and the network in the organisation.
- Stimulate learners to formulate their own goals.
- Brainstorm.

- Be an example of a flexible learner who sees learning opportunities everywhere.
- Avoid traditional lecture rooms with fixed seats as 'the place where learning happens'.
- Let learners influence the content to be learned, the relevance of it and how they will go about it.
- Provide multiple opportunities to learn. Are there ways to access and share information? Do learners have time and space to connect to others and collaborate?
- Recognise, reward and approve learning behaviour explicitly (by supervisors as well as colleagues).
- Do promote teamwork.
- Let your learners build networks and support and encourage this.
- Involve learners in task forces to experience critical incidents, challenges, etc.
- Let learners encounter challenging tasks.
- Remember that experiencing a heavy workload enhances informal learning.
- Remember also that a heavy workload combined with a feeling of not being under control with respect to tasks and timing will result in less investment in learning.
- Create structural opportunities for communication, interaction and cooperation.
- Organise regular meetings where units can meet and consult each other.
- Use trade union meetings as learning opportunities for the participants.
- Share internal job openings.
- Stimulate job rotation.
- Organise common breaks.
- Plan how to onboard new employees.
- Think about the architecture of the workplace in terms of proximity and therefore easy accessibility of colleagues.
- Enhance participation in internal and external networks.
- Plan meetings with external colleagues and visits to other organisations.
- Invite guest speakers.
- Organise communities of practice with external partners.
- Create opportunities for feedback and reflection.
- Use PDPs (personal development plans).
- Implement a buddy system or godfather/godmother system.
- Introduce internships so that new ideas flow into the organisation which trigger employees to reflect.
- Increase the access to information and databases or systems.
- Promote having an idea box.

Build a learning climate

- Install a climate of trust and warmth among colleagues and supervisors.
- Strive for psychological safety when talking about learning.
- Make sure people trust their coworkers/managers enough to firmly state their opinions without repercussion.

- Provide room for making mistakes, sharing them as a first step to reflect on them and learn from them.
- Stimulate critical questioning.
- Give your people time to learn and reward the use of it.
- Allow and trust people to take responsibility in decision-making processes.
- Install learning leadership.
- Let leaders facilitate learning behaviour.
- Let learning leaders promote innovation and risk-taking.
- Share and discuss the results of innovation and risk-taking.
- Ask leaders to be an example of learning while working.
- Ask leaders to share critical learning experiences.
- Create time for analysis and reflection.
- Provide constructive feedback on a regular basis.
- Appreciate and support efforts to learn.
- Provide feedback and rewards for proficiency.
- Stimulate and reward learner agency.

Assessment as Learning

Some programmes do not need any assessment, since no certificates are given. These can surely use assessment as an instrument for learning (Assessment for Learning). Other programmes do assess for learners to earn a certain qualification. In such programmes, there is a risk that assessment becomes the sole focus of the learner and turns all motivation into pure extrinsic motivation. When we were researching professional training programmes in schools, we heard too many students saying 'I only learn when the exam is tomorrow' – a terrifying example of clear extrinsic motivation and no flow in learning. No wonder its impact is limited. That is not what we want, nor is it an ideal situation.

Many researchers have warned about the devastating effect of assessment on learning processes, but turning around such a culture can only be done in a process of drastic turnaround (for a successful example, see Fontys ICT school in Eindhoven).

Assessment as Learning means that…

- assessment is as much situated as the learning;
- assessment can be done by the community/peers/trainers;
- assessment of group learning is as important as the learning of the individual;
- 'in vivo' studies/'live' projects of complex problem-solving provide a richness of information on how a learner is progressing and his or her current level of proficiency.

There are also ways to combine 2G (second generation) and 3G (third generation) assessments such as, for example, two-stage assessments: learners first perform the assessment individually, hand their answers in, and then repeat the assessment in teams. Learners obtain timely feedback from each other and learn from the assessment via discussion and debate with peers. Team results are usually better.

When learners create their own portfolio in order to prove mastery of several competences, it is usually this portfolio evidence that is the starting point for a portfolio assessment dialogue. Of course, it is helpful or indispensable for assessors that the learner adds a reflection paper to the portfolio, providing arguments that underpin the selection of certain evidence for the different specific competences. Our experiences have taught us that portfolios or PDPs can work very well, but a minimum of structuring, guidelines or prescription should be given to the learner.

Assignments worked on during the learning trajectory are also relevant sources of information to track progress in learning. In all of these, exercising 'agency' in the use of resources or tools that provide valid information on your progress as a learner is a key issue in the assessment.

How to increase Assessment as Learning?

How to make assessment a learning experience?

- Enhance strong integration of learning and assessment: learning is a process of continuously updating your competence (knowledge and skills) base, with the assessment of where you are and how you will proceed as important levers for the next step to take.
- Pay attention to the process of learning and not only to the outcomes; the input for improvement lies in both.
- A focus for learning is given by the destination of the learners' journey and precise learning objectives are not tightly pre-specified.
- Aim for an appropriate combination and planning of assessment methods and assessments, preferably continuously.

How to collect information that fuels the learning process?

- Given that learning is an individual as well as collaborative experience, use group assessments as well as individual assessments.
- Use self-, peer-, or co-assessment.
- Use entry-assessment as a starting point to match expectations: dialogue is an important tool to make clear what the starting point is for learning, on which foundations of competences (knowledge and skills) the learner can build.
- Stress inhibits learning: introducing high-stake tests has been proven to induce stress that hinders the learner from performing optimally.
- Reduce testing drastically.
- Use the data available on what learners do during the learning process as an input for the feedback dialogue with the learner (portfolios; PDPs).
- Stimulate learners to proactively seek the feedback they need; support the learners in developing an attitude of feedback-seeking.

- Make asking and giving feedback an attitude: feedup (where are you going to?), feedback (how did it go?), feedforward (how will you proceed?).
- Increase peer assessments, in order to attain a natural habit of learning from each other and to show interest in the work of others.
- Let learners discuss how to operationalise the evaluation criteria for peer assessment.
- Avoid formative or diagnostic 'tests': they are usually summative; instead, provide constructive feedback constantly during meetings.
- Use portfolio assessments.
- Introduce competence logs.
- If you have good arguments for administering a summative test, introduce two-stage assessments (first an individual assignment; then hand this in; then work on that same assignment in teams; and hand it in).
- Use products as input for assessment.
- Determine criteria in interaction with learners.
- Use self-assessment.
- Use 180-degree feedback as a tool.
- Use 360-degree feedback as a tool for learning and assessment.
- Implement 3G assessment: how well do people exercise 'agency' in their use of the resources or tools available to them to formulate problems, work productively and evaluate their efforts?
- Ask learners to document the feedback they received (to monitor progress).
- 'In vivo' studies/'live' projects of complex problem-solving offer ample information on how the learner is doing.
- Audio and video recordings are useful tools to provide information on the progress of the learner.

Other issues to think about

- Evaluation needs to be more holistic.
- Assessment as Learning based on ongoing performance or 'exit' exhibitions.
- Learners work across disciplines.
- Learners or instructors both can devise a task.
- Learners practise using accumulated knowledge and apply it to new situations.
- Learners engage in effective communication in oral, written and visual forms.
- Reflections of learners are taken into account.

5

WHY CAN THEY DO WHAT WE CANNOT?

Ten secrets of future learning in top training programmes

Looking at the High Impact Learning building blocks, the first question that readers ask us is mostly related to competitors: Can they do this? Do they realise all of the building blocks in their Learning and Development (L&D) programmes? What is their secret? What does an organisation that is future-learning-proof look like?

Over the past few years, we have scrutinised how such organisations work. We camped next door and followed their activities through not only document and content analyses, but also through observations and interviews with the management, trainers, teachers and learners.

Ten key boosters

What is the secret of successful High Impact Learning that Lasts (HILL)? Here are the ten key boosters:

1 Teamwork

L&D professionals, teachers, trainers and the management work in strong interaction and in teams. The whole L&D team, the teaching team or the corporate university staff members work as a team with a high level of information sharing and interdependency.

2 A shared vision

A shared vision within the team that originates from the bottom up, and is shared by all layers in the organisation. In successful HILL organisations, it is surprising but encouraging to see that all layers (management, L&D professionals, learners) have, independent of their role, a similar vision of learning and development and the approach to realise this. This vision is an integral part of the organisational culture. It acts like a part of the brand box: new employees are attracted to join the organisation since learning is an asset. All participants feel good in their own skin and feel that there is space for individual development. All are engaged to work on this vision and to continuously adapt the shared vision to new developments.

3 Continuous 'engineering' of their approach and L&D programme

Learners continuously learn from colleagues; middle management, teachers and trainers regularly update learning trajectories and approaches (rethinking parts of the training programmes, and optimising and innovating these). There is a tendency towards innovation and creating challenges oneself.

4 Teachers/trainers learn continuously from learners

'Reciprocal teaching', or perhaps even better, 'reciprocal learning', is practised as much as possible. Teachers and trainers see themselves as learners and try to develop themselves further. They share their know-how and ask learners to search for information and share it. As such, a culture of continuously looking for new information is cultivated. Knowledge is built in teams and applied to new challenging situations. Learners adapt to creating new knowledge for future situations. Strong involvement is a guarantee for a strong knowledge base and future adaptation to new situations.

5 Continuous feedback to learners and between learners

Both practice and learning sciences have shown for a long time that providing constructive feedback creates a strong and effective learning moment. But practice also shows that many programmes lack serious and good feedback-giving. In successful HILL programmes, there is an atmosphere of continuously steering feedback that becomes the norm. Helping each other in learning new things, sharing ideas, discussing failures, being surprised and explaining this to others, mutual constructive feedback between learners, strong feedback-seeking, and urging colleagues to engage in the learning process are the key boosters of learning.

6 Communities of learning and teams that create short communication lines, support each other and enable a lot of sharing

Teams create their own dynamics. They have autonomy and learners take on responsibilities. Communities promote knowledge sharing, making progress, and boundary-crossing communication and actions. In successful HILL organisations, the jargon follows the culture: concepts such as 'training', 'classrooms' and 'lectures' disappear; instead, **the era of 'labs'** is entered: all sources communicate terms such as 'change labs', 'transformation labs', 'learning labs', 'facilitators', 'just-in-time expert e-sessions', 'knowledge e-clips', 'co-labs', 'co-construction labs', 'exploration labs', 'experience labs', 'work labs', etc. We are certainly convinced that changing the complete organisational jargon is a facilitating factor in realising innovation.

7 Trust in the learners and a development-oriented approach

All L&D programmes communicate a strong belief in the talents of all participants. This supports the self-efficacy of learners and empowers them. In practice, it results in providing learners with responsibilities in performing complex tasks or projects and searching for information to do so as a part of personal development.

8 Learning is a central issue in creating future competitiveness

Learning is seen as central for building the future competitiveness of the organisation. The brand box of the organisation holds no material rewards, but rather L&D vouchers as rewards.

9 A focus on problem-solving and reflection of learners

Successful High Impact Learning is boosted by a clear focus on continuous problem-solving, both by learners and coaches, in order to solve problems that are relevant to the learner, to the organisation or to current society. Learners learn to solve future problems when reflecting on the problem-solving process they go through: How are we doing now? Are we doing well? Why did we make these choices? What were the steps we took? Can we do better? How? Should we do it differently next time? Why? etc.

10 Learners are aware that they steer their own development

The established learning culture results in the habit that people learn continuously and that learners realise that they steer their own development since there is an atmosphere that provides the necessary incentives to do this. This ensures a knowledgeable, competent, agile and reflective workforce for the future.

Reaching these ten goals in your organisation

If you are striving to implement these ten goals in your own organisation, there are basically three issues to tackle: **strategy**, **leadership**, and **learning climate**. These form the underlying conditions for a smooth implementation of HILL.

Strategy: Aligning strategy and L&D

Organisations are required to constantly realign their strategy to fit the changing circumstances if they want to successfully compete in increasingly competitive markets. In order to develop the capabilities necessary to execute the newly acquired strategic plan, businesses progressively depend on their employees' knowledge as their most valuable asset. When the business strategy changes, organisations are often required to reformulate which competences are indispensable. Consequently, L&D activities and practices need to be aligned with the overall business strategy to ensure that employees are trained and develop those newly required competences. Although the importance of alignment is recognised widely, it is difficult to achieve given that the business strategy is constantly changing.

Different departments, however, might only pursue their own interests, which possibly deviate from the interest of the organisation as a whole, hindering an organisation-wide alignment of learning practices. A lack of a common view of the strategy among key players (management team, trainers, teachers, L&D, middle management) who are responsible for the implementation of L&D policies and practices can prevent the development of common purpose and commitment, which is also the case at lower levels. Consequently, it can be assumed that employees establish a divergent understanding of what is expected from them and which capabilities to develop to meet those expectations, hindering an organisation-wide alignment of L&D policies and, therefore, organisational learning. If the understanding of the strategic goals differs among employees, uncertainty increases, leading to a stronger possibility of employees relying on their own interpretations and thus disparate and possibly contradicting policies and practices. Thus, a shared understanding of the strategy and its implications for L&D is necessary at all levels of the organisation for successful transformation according to the new acquired organisational goals. But how can organisations ensure the development of shared understanding?

By providing a setting in which individuals can engage in a free flow of meaning and exploration of their personal predispositions, employees will become aware of the process through which they form assumptions. Such interaction establishes an understanding of how collective thinking and feelings evolve and so develops common strengths and capabilities for working together. Creating common paradigms and the development of a common understanding of the strategy can be assumed to support employees in taking common action, leading to a quicker alignment of L&D practices to changes in the strategy. Research found evidence of relations between dialogue interventions and the degree of goal coherence within and between teams.

The importance of linking L&D practices and policies with the strategy to foster flexibility and, therefore, pave the way for organisational change, is widely recognised, bringing L&D departments to the forefront of organisational transformation. In this respect, the concept of strategic L&D has been put forward. Strategic L&D is defined as the practice of aligning and integrating L&D policies and practices with the overall organisational strategy, so that the organisation's human capital most effectively contributes to its strategic objectives. As organisations are competing in a global economy, and are increasingly focused on knowledge-based work, they strive to differentiate on the basis of the skills, knowledge and motivation of their workforce. This requires the role of L&D to be strategic, indicating the necessity of L&D policies for organisational branding and both attracting and retaining the workforce, and practices being aligned with the business strategy by assessing the current capabilities, what is needed and providing the knowledge, skills and attitudes (KSAs) for the unknown future.

Leadership for Learning

It not only recognised that organisational structures which support the collective development of L&D practices and policies between HR and business units play a crucial role in establishing strategic learning practices. Leadership practices, such as transformational or transactional leadership, are also widely acknowledged to support the alignment of L&D as they play a crucial role in the translation of the strategic changes to the employees.

Over the last four decades, researchers have studied leadership and more general leadership models applied in learning organisations. The results of these numerous studies on various leadership theories have begun to show fairly consistent patterns and resulted in the emergence of the Leadership for Learning theory. Leadership for Learning integrates features of transformational leadership and distributed or shared leadership.

Leadership for Learning is team-oriented or collaborative and refers to organisation-wide leadership by those in formal management roles and by those in less formal management roles, e.g. trainers, programme directors, coordinators, employees, students.

Secondly, Leadership for Learning has an explicit focus on the performance of the employee/learner and aims to impact the organisational outcomes through creating and sustaining an organisation-wide focus on learning, i.e. a learning climate. The focus on achievement relates to capacity-building as the third feature of Leadership for Learning. Capacity-building subsumes strategy or actions taken to increase the collective efficacy to improve performance of the learners through new knowledge, enhanced resources and greater motivation both individually and together. Such capacity-building is also demanding but it allows every member of the organisation to learn and to contribute, so it benefits its sustainability.

Our own research on Leadership for Learning shows that leaders that stress the professional development of their people distinguish themselves from leaders that see learning as a individual issue (e.g. Baars et al., 2017). Successful leaders pay more attention to organisational culture and strive for a shared vision. They stimulate cooperation through stimulating responsibility for innovative projects. They create facilities for social informal learning through supporting individuals. They function as a coach, try to be a role model and see the talents of employees. The results show that providing professional development trajectories is necessary but not sufficient; creating possibilities for collaboration within the organisation with colleagues is essential for learning. This interaction with colleagues is the source for information, seeking help and feedback, reflection on processes and practice, and as such is essential leverage for cultivating a learning climate based on a shared vision, where people share thoughts about what is going right and wrong, about strengths and weaknesses, opportunities and threats.

Learning climate – a climate for learning

Interaction and shared vision not only requires open communication but also a supportive climate, which allows a free flow of information without negative consequences.

Such a supportive climate can be enhanced, as stated earlier, by changing all traditional concepts in a learning organisation, such as 'training, lesson, lesson plan, teacher, trainer, academy', etc. into jargon that resembles the real workplace more. Currently, we see that many L&D programmes take this advice for granted and have entered the 'era of labs'. There is a lab for everything, and I mostly like such concepts since they announce a change in view, a change in mindset and consequently a change in the way of working and learning. Young employees nowadays seem to value the chances provided for learning and personal development more than their current salary. And this trend seems to be continuing. Installing a climate for learning may become the most important factor in competing for excellent employees as a crucial part of your brand box.

Organisations that work with HILL or prepare to ground their L&D in the HILL approach are mostly characterised by an excellent learning climate or should prepare to have such a climate.

A climate for learning is the collection of the issue-specific observable perceptions shared among organisational members about what helps and hinders learning

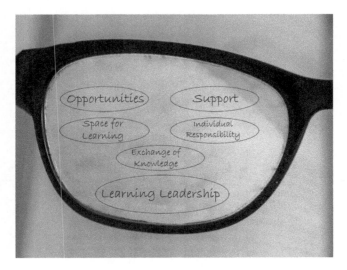

FIGURE 5.1 A climate for learning – components (Emonds et al., 2017)

for the individual as well as for the organisation itself (and the meaning attached to those perceptions of the policies, practices and procedures of the work environment provided). This means that climate can be measured through the individual perceptions of the learning environment (Emonds et al., 2017). Of course, it is through social interactions and the creation of similar personal values that individual perceptions come closer together and ultimately become shared among teams, employees, learners and organisations.

Such a climate for learning is directly observable, measurable, cyclical (perceptions constitute the climate and climate influences perceptions) and thus temporal. Finally, a climate for learning is multi-dimensional. The Climate for Learning Model of Emonds et al. (2017) visualises these dimensions (see Figure 5.1).

TABLE 5.1

Fuelling a learning climate

Provide opportunities to learn	Give your people opportunities to develop and grow. Are there ways to access and share information and do you give them time and space to connect to others and collaborate?
Provide support	Do you recognise, reward and approve learning behaviour? Do you celebrate learning successes? Are you facilitating support? Are you giving people your trust and warmth? Is there psychological safety when people are talking about learning? Do people firmly state their opinions without repercussions?
Provide space for learning	Is there time for learning? Can they plan time in their agenda? And a learning space? Are there any constraints that people will be facing if they plan to learn? Do you work on removing this?
Take (and give!) individual responsibility for learning	Do people get individual responsibility? Can they take decisions? Is there participative decision-making? Do you trust people with the autonomy to make decisions about their learning?
Enhance knowledge exchange	Is dialogue and (constructive) conflict stimulated? How do people talk to each other? Are they seeing learning opportunities in failure? Are they exchanging valuable information they learned?
Provide learning leadership	Are your leaders facilitating learning behaviour and supporting it in their daily life? Are they promoting innovation and risk-taking? Are the results of innovation and risk-taking shared and discussed? This can be called the basis of a learning climate: leaders acting as such build a foundation for a learning organisation with impact!

Considering these findings and the existence of an interrelationship between climate and communication, it can be assumed that open communication, supported by climate, can enhance the shared understanding of what an organisation expects from its employees. In short, open communication is said to improve the strategic alignment of L&D practices with the organisational strategy as it fosters shared understanding. This in turn stimulates L&D executives, HR professionals, teachers and trainers to collectively adapt practices and policies, which in turn guides employees to collectively adapt their learning activities to the capabilities that are needed for the organisation to keep up standards.

6

APPLICATIONS OF HILL

CASE 1: SCIENTOR N.V. AND SCIENTOR ACADEMY: AN APPLICATION OF HIGH IMPACT LEARNING THAT LASTS[1]

EXECUTIVE SUMMARY

As the technical sector is changing rapidly nowadays, knowledge is becoming obsolete quickly. This is also the case for Scientor N.V., a technical company facing strong international competition and therefore being continuously challenged to innovate. In this context, in order to keep the knowledge up to date, the continuous earning of all employees is of utmost importance to Scientor. The Scientor Academy is responsible for designing and providing training in order to realise High Impact Learning. To what extent are the current Learning and Development (L&D) practices at Scientor HILL-proof? Or, to what extent do Scientor employees engage in learning activities that contribute to the development, fine-tuning, broadening and deepening of knowledge skills and attitudes and, in turn, support them to create or increase significant and unique value for his/her job and the organisation? Do the learning activities facilitated and supported by the

Scientor Academy enrich the body of knowledge, skills and attitudes (KSAs) of the employees in such a way that the learner's professional functioning improves and consequently influences future situations in his/her working context?

By means of interviews with individual employees and focus group interviews, the current learning situation is analysed according to the building blocks of the HILL approach. The main findings are described for each of the following building blocks.

- **Urgency, Gap, Problem:** There is a sense of urgency for learning which usually evolves from individual employees,employees that are lacking knowledge at the start of a project, or from Scientor's strategic goals of becoming a world leader. Nevertheless, few L&D activities start clearly from a predefined problem or a clearly expressed urgency by employees and training is still the predominant form of L&D activity.
- **Learner Agency:** Most employees at Scientor should be proactive in taking responsibility and initiative for their own learning process.
- **Collaboration and Coaching:** Employees are aware of the importance of learning from others and cooperating on the job. Some coaching and buddy systems are in place but lie outside the responsibility of the Academy. Line managers would like to coach employees. However, they feel restricted due to time constraints and conflicting responsibilities.
- **Hybrid Learning:** Currently, the Academy uses blended learning by combining different methods and e-learning with classroom training. This should be extended to more hybrid learning, a well-thought-out balance between online and face-to-face learning. Employees would appreciate more opportunities for follow-up and reflection after a training programme.
- **Action and Knowledge Sharing:** Training programmes are not always offered in time. Knowledge sharing happens accidently in or between some teams but not in a structured way.
- **Flexibility – Formal and Informal Learning:** In general, people are willing to learn formally and informally. The culture is open and people are eager to learn. Often, new and senior employees collaborate closely. However, learning activities can be constrained due to time pressure. Furthermore, it is up to line managers whether they take initiatives to enhance learning. Some of them will do this; many do not.
- **Assessment as Learning:** Learning at Scientor N.V. is seen as an employee's responsibility. According to the stakeholders, managers provide guidance regarding learning needs. Discussions about the employee's learning process is not seen as the line manager's responsibility. Due to the high priority of projects, feedback is mostly given regarding job performance. Thus, assessment of process and products is mostly used for measuring performance, while it could also be used as a learning event.

After analysing the current situation, recommendations on how to foster the impact of learning are given.

1. Introduction

Every year, billions of euros are spent on training and development programmes for employees in organisations throughout Europe. However, what happens after the training is most of the time out of scope for many organisations. This poses a challenge to companies, especially those who operate in the technological sector. The technology sector, like any other sector, is nowadays constantly changing at a fast pace. Changes are inevitable and consequently learning plays a crucial role as knowledge is becoming obsolete quickly. In order to keep skills and knowledge up to date, learning has to take place throughout people's entire careers. However, the core question is: does the investment in L&D result in impactful learning? Only then can we expect supporting the L&D of employees to be an example of a human resource intervention that contributes to the competitive advantage of an organisation (Bartlett, 2001). This is the context in which Scientor N.V. is operating and the challenges the company is facing.

1.1 Company background

Scientor N.V. produces systems and technical supplies for the airline industry and parcel and post solutions for customers worldwide. The systems are used in airports all over the world, by the biggest parcel and postal companies, and in leading European e-commerce firms. Furthermore, Scientor N.V. is a global market leader with a yearly turnover of about 4 billion euros. Worldwide, Scientor N.V. employs more than 3,150 employees in various functions. The number of employees is increasing steadily. Offices and customer centres, software houses, and manufacturing sites are located in 16 countries around the globe.

As a technical company Scientor N.V. is facing fierce international competition in the high-tech market. There is a great need for innovation to stay ahead of the competition. Therefore, learning activities within Scientor N.V. play a crucial role. The Scientor Academy (hereinafter Academy), which was established in 2008, is the department responsible for training employees and facilitating learning in all global divisions. In total, eight employees take care of the learning needs within Scientor N.V. The Academy offers a wide range of learning activities, ranging from soft skills such as communication skills to the hard skills provided in technical training programmes. In order to provide specialised learning activities, the Academy works with external partners who have specific knowledge on certain topics. Also, learning activities are coached by employees of the Academy. Furthermore, the Academy trains Scientor N.V. employees to become internal trainers.

1.2 Scientor's problem

Currently for Scientor N.V., the bottleneck in their growth is to ensure that new people are efficient in their daily work a short period of time after their initial training. Many companies aim for their learning interventions such as training programmes having a high impact. However, the focus on the process after a training programme is minimal and transferring the new knowledge to the work environment is usually not taken into consideration. The Academy has acknowledged this and sees room for improvement concerning the transfer of learning and therefore the impact of the learning activities it provides. If the Academy improves the impact of their L&D offer, they can improve their support to Scientor N.V.'s rapid pace of growth. The Academy realised that one way to achieve higher impact of their L&D offer would be to implement the HILL model.

More concretely, in order to make sure that the learning interventions of the Academy have a high impact, the learners need to be able to transfer what has been learned to the workplace. To facilitate this learning transfer, the insights on High Impact Learning are seen as helpful.

2. Case analysis

The core question of this case analysis is:

> *What actions can the Academy undertake to foster transfer of learning, based on the High Impact Learning that Lasts (HILL) approach?*

In order to answer this core question, two subquestions are tackled:

> What is the current situation within Scientor N.V. when it is analysed according to the HILL approach?
> What are short- and long-term recommendations for the Academy in order to achieve High Impact Learning that Lasts?

2.1 Question 1: Where do we stand now? How HILL-proof are we?

In order to answer this question, individual interviews and four focus group interviews were conducted with the HR director, the Talent Development department, employees, trainers, line managers and HR managers.

Building block 1: Urgency, gap, problem

A sense of urgency can evolve at Scientor N.V. in three ways.

First, a sense of urgency most often arises at the start of a project. In this phase a lack of knowledge and/or skills is identified. Adequate skills and knowledge are seen as a prerequisite for the success of the project and are facilitated by learning activities. However, employees and trainers both noted that sometimes training programmes on hard skills are not provided in time. For example, an employee noted that he or she needed training urgently but it could not be provided at that time. When it was possible to join the training programme, it was no longer needed as the employee had already acquired the skills somewhere else. The trainers also noted that in some cases people have been on a waiting list for two years. This could lead to a situation where the employee does not need the training any more because the skills are acquired in another way. This problem is most eminent for technical or hard skills training and the introductory training. For soft skills training this is less of a problem as employees think that they are less time-bound.

Second, employees sometimes identify a general gap in their knowledge or behaviour that is not bounded to a specific task. This is usually associated with personal development. A manager could help to identify gaps by discussing the performance of an employee; however, at Scientor N.V. managers mainly help employees to identify learning needs when they underperform or they only address the high performers. For instance, one participant of the HR focus group stated: 'it is only for the talents or the guys who need the attention, positive or negative'.

Lastly, a sense of urgency arises from the strategy and the vision of Scientor N.V. As Scientor N.V. wants to become a market leader and to achieve fast growth growth in a short period of time, the employees feel that it is important to keep their knowledge up to date. As the high-tech industry is highly complex, competitive and fast-moving, Scientor N.V. is dependent on a quick integration of new employees and continuous learning of current employees. All stakeholders seem to acknowledge that it is crucial for newly hired people to gain knowledge and skills that are important for them to perform their job quickly and without making too many errors.

In general, we observed that employees in all layers of the organisation value learning and see its importance. Nevertheless, not all L&D activities start clearly from a predefined problem or a clearly expressed urgency by employees, and training is still the predominant form of L&D activities.

Building block 2: Learner agency

Overall, people at Scientor N.V. do think that learning is their own responsibility and that they have to take initiative to learn themselves; as an employee stated: 'you need to be proactive, yes, learn yourself'. A proactive attitude is therefore necessary to learn within Scientor N.V. However, less proactive people might be more reluctant to share their learning needs and might fall behind. The employees proposed that a manager would be of help in this situation to initiate the learning process. For example, the manager should use a personal development plan (PDP) that stimulates the learners to think about learning and to take action themselves.

The L&D activities and training in particular show a very low level of learner agency. The influence of the learner is low and choices for employees within the sessions are restricted. The general feeling is still that they 'undergo' training, instead of 'steering themselves' through the training or L&D activity.

Building block 3: Collaboration and coaching

During the interviews and focus groups, it became clear that most stakeholders of the Academy are aware of the importance of collaboration and social interaction in the workplace. Therefore, related programmes such as coaching or buddy systems are put in place. The coaching system is taken care of by the Talent Development department, which matches learners and coaches according to their learning needs. Coaches are either externally hired, which is mostly the case if specific skills or knowledge are not available within Scientor N.V., or internally hired (e.g. very experienced employees). In addition, line managers feel that they take on a coaching role; however, they cannot coach their employees objectively because they are also involved in appraising the employees.

Another way in which collaboration and social interaction is facilitated within Scientor N.V. is via buddy systems. In these systems, learners are paired up with other participants in a training programme or with a colleague so that they can help each other out and learn from each other's experiences. The pairing up between learner and participant could happen formally as part of a training programme or informally at the workplace. However, the HR focus group revealed that the use of any coaching or buddy systems depends on the initiative of an individual. First, learners have to know of its existence and, secondly, they have to want to take part in it.

Furthermore, line managers take on a supporting role when it comes to the learning process of their employees. However, the focus groups revealed that line managers consider their responsibility to be mainly before the start of a training programme, and less during and after the training. In contrast, the Talent Development department sees the involvement of line managers as important in all stages – namely, before, during and after the training. Interestingly, it seems that the employees generally view their line managers as crucial to their personal long-term development while they perceive their project leaders as more important for their functional development. However, involving line managers seems to be challenging, but is necessary in practice due to the presence of time constraints and a lack of close cooperation between line management and the Academy.

Finally, within the current L&D activities that are predominantly classical training, the level of cooperation and small-group work/learning is very low or even non-existent.

Building block 4: Hybrid learning

As Scientor N.V. uses a combination of learning methods and of e-learning and classroom learning, their design can be defined as blended.

Within the focus groups it became apparent that HR has the feeling that many employees are not aware of Scientor N.V.'s e-learning possibilities and the internal Wikipedia system. Moreover, the learners would appreciate being able to use e-learning more frequently – for instance, when dealing with cross-national learning issues. Often, training participants from outside the country do not come back to the headquarters for follow-ups and other events. In this respect, both the employees and trainers felt that the Academy could increase the usage of e-learning when developing training programmes, as one of the employees illustrated: 'keeping internationalisation in mind during e-learning is very valuable'.

In sum, hybrid learning, as a well-thought-out balance between online and offline learning, is not yet in place and needs to be worked on in order to increase impact and time-efficiency for the future.

Building block 5: Action and knowledge sharing

Employees noted that training programmes are generally not useful. Knowledge sharing happens during most training sessions between the participants and the trainer, less obviously among participants, and hardly ever before or after the sessions. Employees closely cooperate on the job and therefore debate with each other to communicate and share knowledge, to some extent.

Further, in technical training programmes, employees feel that the information given is not very specific to their job. The trainers also acknowledged that training programmes are sometimes too general and give no room for actively practising the skills needed daily. Although employees are aware that a training programme cannot be tailored to everyone individually, they would be interested in having practical cases or simulations incorporated in the training that reflect their daily tasks on the job and where they can practise together. This would make it easier for them to apply the new knowledge after the training. In addition, they would like to have the opportunity to ask questions to their colleagues who have participated in the training as well as the trainer when they apply the knowledge and skills in practice after the training.

Building block 6: Flexibility – formal and informal

The focus groups described the organisational mindset towards learning as open and that people are eager to learn. Colleagues on the work floor help each other when necessary and new employees closely collaborate with more senior employees who sometimes act as a coach or mentor. However, time can be an issue with regard to on-the-job learning. Often, especially during a project, there is no time for experimentation and learning. Some managers do schedule meetings for discussion, brainstorming or feedback but this is not implemented by everyone. Thus, in general, the organisation is open to learning formally as well as informally, but a lack of time or the focus on deadlines can hinder the ability to learn on the job.

Moreover, more boundary-crossing is needed to enhance learning from each other as part of the daily work. Composing task- or project-related groups of experienced workers and newcomers, groups of participants with different backgrounds and disciplinary competences, would enhance informal learning opportunities and in turn optimise work efficiency and effectiveness.

Building block 7: Assessment as Learning

Learning at Scientor N.V. is mainly seen as the employees' responsibility. Most stakeholders perceive it as the line manager's responsibility to ensure transfer of the acquired skills and knowledge and remind employees after training programmes of what they have learned. However, the line managers themselves do not see this as their responsibility. Because of the high priority of projects, feedback is mostly given regarding job performance. This happens twice a year with an individual evaluation and appraisal meeting. Thus, assessment is currently used for measuring performance rather than using it as a learning moment or trying to measure what was learned from specific learning activities, and thus stimulating follow-up and transfer. Giving feedback more regularly only happens at the initiative of the line manager. Therefore, it is not at all consistently present in the entire organisation.

In this respect, in order to bridge the gap between learning and application at the workplace, the employees indicated that they would like to practise and reflect much more on the skills they learned during training programmes. Some employees referred to the Pit-Stop follow-up as a good example. However, they felt that reflection is missing in many training programmes. They differentiated between soft skills training and hard skills training interventions. When it comes to soft skills they appreciate moments of interaction with others, possibilities to reflect on what was learned, and follow-up meetings that should take place within half a year after the training. With regard to hard skills training, the employees like to do practical assignments so that additional or more specific knowledge can be gained. Additionally, they would like follow-up sessions shortly after the training so that knowledge is not forgotten and they are able to ask questions that evolved on the job.

During the interviews, it also became apparent that making mistakes is generally accepted at Scientor. It seems that on an individual level, people learn from their mistakes and know how to deal with them. It should be noted that in the interviews we conducted, we only spoke to people of the same nationality. Some stakeholders stated that they know that making mistakes might be perceived differently by workers from other nationalities. For example, some Asian workers may consider asking questions or admitting mistakes as a sign of incompetence. This makes it more difficult to learn from mistakes and inhibits the learning process. Additionally, some stakeholders noted that compared to individuals, the organisation as a whole does not learn from mistakes very well. It was explained that the lessons learned from mistakes in one country are currently not shared throughout the entire organisation. This leads to the occurrence of similar mistakes in other countries, which is costly and inefficient. Overall, this is a challenge on a global scale for Scientor and the Academy.

Summary of HILL analysis

As a summary of the current state of the art of HILL at Scientor, a visual indication of the current situation regarding the HILL approach is shown in Figure 6.1. It is based on our interpretation of the findings that were described in the previous chapter. The shades of grey indicate how well on track the current situation is for

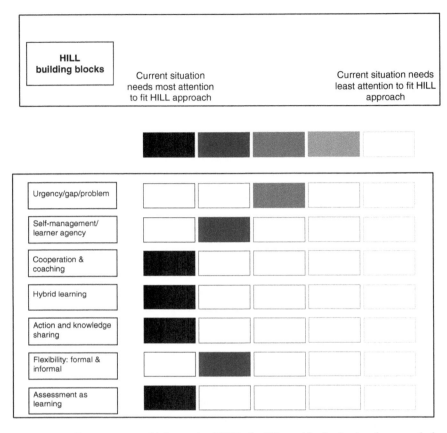

FIGURE 6.1 Degree to which each HILL building block is implemented by Scientor N.V.

each building block and how much room for growth there still is. We recommend gradually optimising the L&D practices, by first focusing on the building blocks that need most improvement. In addition, Scientor should continue building on the foundation that is already there and adjust, optimise and put emphasis on the right components to strengthen the impact. Therefore, our short-term recommendations elaborated upon in the next section are focused on the building blocks that currently show most potential for growth. In Figure 6.1, the shading indicates how HILL-proof Scientor is right now. The very light grey colour indicates that the current situation needs the least attention; however, the Academy should continue working on this to maintain this situation and to avoid deterioration. The black colour indicates high importance of the specific building block to work on. The grey colour shows which building blocks need attention in the near future but are less urgent than the black-coloured building blocks. The black to white continuum shows a decreasing urgency for the need to pay attention.

Looking at the current situation from a HILL perspective, it is clear that Scientor N.V. is already doing a reasonable job on a few of the building blocks while many others still have a lot of potential for improvement. The first building block, sense of urgency, is given some attention within Scientor. The third, fourth, fifth and seventh building blocks need much more attention. Also building blocks two and six still have room for improvement. However, focusing on building block 3, 4, 5 and 7 has more short-term potential for improvement. Therefore, the recommendations for short-term actions are based on these four building blocks.

2.2 Basic conditions: 'to build up high, the foundation needs to be solid'

During the project, we discovered some issues that, strictly speaking, would be out of the scope of the current project. However, they were mentioned frequently throughout the interviews and focus groups and led to the golden principle 'to build up high, the foundation needs to be solid'. If the basic conditions are not acted upon, the proposed short-term interventions for making Scientor more HILL-proof will not be as successful and will not have the intended high impact that is aimed for. Therefore, we will briefly describe the basis success conditions and provide preliminary ideas on how to improve them. In total, we discovered five challenges for the Academy: the marketing of the Academy; cooperation with the Talent Development department and the rest of the HR department; clarity on the allocation of the budget; focusing on the core activities of the Academy; and the responsibility for transfer of learning.

Basic condition 1: Marketing

Not all people in the organisation are aware of the Academy's offerings and respon-sibilities. With respect to the latter, the distinction between the Academy and the Talent Development department is not clear. Concerning the portfolio of services provided by the Academy, it is suggested that the Academy should create more awareness of their offerings and promote their services within the company. A pos-sible way to do so is by creating a poster or a visual to show what the Academy offers, and to spread this throughout the company. Furthermore, an infographic could be developed and sent to all employees worldwide to raise awareness of learning pos-sibilities. Thereby, the Academy would increasingly be perceived as an international support service of training within Scientor. To strengthen this approach, it could make use of international ambassadors who promote the services of the Academy in their subsidiaries. Another possibility is that the Academy and the international ambassadors could use their personal networks to promote the Academy's work. Additionally, they could set up lunch meetings and e-meetings for everyone who is interested in knowing more about the offerings of the Academy. This informal setting would offer the possibility to get to know the Academy and ask ques-tions about learning activities and how to apply for training. Lastly, the intranet of

Scientor could be used more to make employees aware of the Academy and their offerings through news posts or a webpage where all the information about the Academy is accessible to all employees.

Basic condition 2: Cooperation with the Talent Development department and HR

This issue is intertwined with the previous one. The division of responsibilities and tasks between the HR department, the Talent Development department and the Academy should be clear-cut and communicated throughout the organisation. For example, it should be clear who is in charge of analysing learning questions. Thereby, people know to whom they need to turn to with their questions and, therefore, extra and double work could be avoided. Furthermore, our interviews and focus groups showed that there are ways in which especially the Talent Development department and the Academy can cooperate and help each other. Closer cooperation is already foreseen in the HR strategy. Another suggestion is that the existing informal buddy and formal coaching system could be used as tools by the Academy to ensure that people who followed a training programme have someone they can turn to. In order to do so, the Academy would need access to the pool of coaches of the Talent Development department. The new office building of Scientor offers further possibilities for cooperation between the two departments and the HR department overall. If they could be located close to each other, exchange about best practices could be fostered and, thereby, those departments could learn from each other more easily. Moreover, it would also help to align the procedural parts such as the planning and administration of the Talent Development department with the Academy. In this way synergies would be created, which could be exploited by the involved parties.

Basic condition 3: Clarity on L&D budgets

Questions such as 'who pays for what part of the training design process?' were raised by several stakeholders. A consequence of this lack of clarity could be misunderstandings and confusion as to who takes on the costs and who is paid for what. This leads to feelings of frustration for all parties involved in the long haul and should be avoided. Therefore, as a third basic success factor it is recommended to create and communicate a clear and understandable overview of who is responsible for covering which costs in the training design process. To create a mutual understanding of the value of a proper training design budget, it could be helpful to disseminate an information sheet that contains an overview of what costs and efforts are required to design a certain training programme. In this way, expectations can be managed for all parties and awareness can be raised of the importance of a proper training budget that covers all costs. Managers and middle managers might feel less reluctant to invest in a training programme if they know what they are paying for or what it takes in terms of time, effort and resources (human and material), and in turn in budget, to design a high-quality programme.

Basic condition 4: Back to the core

For every organisation it is essential to concentrate on its core activities. These activities are the ones an organisation is most proficient in and they are the most valuable as well, in terms of profit and positive image-building. This principle is applicable to the Academy too. The expertise of the Academy lies in facilitating high-quality and solid formal learning activities that keep the Scientor employees up-to-date in the rapidly changing industry they are in. According to the HR strategy, this is the Academy's core activity and serves to reach the main goal of 'getting the best out of our employees'. Facilitating these learning activities is crucial to maintain the global market leader position within the industry. However, during the interviews it was noted that the workload that comes with this responsibility brings with it a substantial amount of pressure for the employees of the Academy. To relieve these employees from some of this pressure and thereby strengthening the focus and manpower towards the Academy's core activity, we recommend handing over to another department within Scientor satellite tasks such as promotion of Scientor at schools and fairs. The additional time that will become available can provide an opportunity for the Academy to focus on more learning questions and become even better at what it does best: facilitating learning for everyone within Scientor.

Basic condition 5: Responsibility for transfer of learning

As stated earlier, transfer of learning is a process that starts before a learning activity begins and it continues during and after a learning activity. Consequently, facilitating transfer of what is learned into the workplace is the responsibility of every person who is involved in the learning process of an individual. For the Academy, this means that it can really make a difference for the impact of its learning activities in the workplace by stimulating, supporting and guiding the right people at the right moment in the learning process. By actively steering transfer of learning, the Academy can enhance the added value of its training. More specific actions on how the Academy could support the key players in taking responsibility for transfer in different phases of the learning process are elaborated on in the next section.

Summary of the five basic conditions

The Academy should act upon five basic conditions to make sure their L&D interventions will have the targeted effect. These conditions are:

- marketing of the Academy within Scientor;
- closer cooperation between the Academy, the Talent Development department and the other parts of HR;
- clarification of the responsibility and allocation process of training budgets;
- more focus on the core activities of the Academy;
- more responsibility for learning impact and transfer.

2.3 Question 2: What are short- and long-term recommendations for the Academy in order to achieve High Impact Learning that Lasts?

Start moving

This section includes short-term recommendations that are based on the HILL approach, specific actions which aim at increasing the lasting impact of their training programmes.

Figure 6.2 indicates when exactly the Academy should initiate the individual actions and which building blocks are involved. Overall, the specific interventions that are described in the following will result in impactful learning.

Some of the actions proposed in Figure 6.2 start in the indicated phase (before, during, after), but have more impact when they are continued during the following phases. Figure 6.2 also shows when to start and which actions to continue during the next phases.

Figure 6.3 shows when the short-term interventions take place.

Before Training		During Training		After Training	
Actions	**HILL blocks**	**Actions**	**HILL blocks**	**Actions**	**HILL blocks**
Involvement of line manager	3	Assign co-learner	3,4,5	Update line manager	3,5,7
Choose 'support giver'	3	Define plan for practical assignment	4	Connect learner with experienced colleague	3,5
Learner community	3,4,5	Visual reminders & postcards	4	Sharing lessons learned in casual setting	3,4,5
Bring real-life example	5	In-between reflection	4,5,7	Follow-up meetings	4,5,7
				Apply plan and getting feedback	4,7

FIGURE 6.2 Start moving towards HILL

Interventions	Time period of action		
	Before training	During training	After training
Involvement of line manager	■		
Choose 'support giver'	■		■
Learner community	■	■	
Bring real-life example	■	■	■
Assign co-learner		■	
Define plan for practical assignment		■	
Visual reminder and postcards		■	
In-between reflection		■	
Update line manager			■
Connect learner with experienced colleague			■
Sharning lessons learned in casual setting			■
Follow-up meetings			■
Apply plan and get feedback			■

FIGURE 6.3 Short–term interventions

Actions to take before the training starts

The period before the training is important, as good preparation is half of the work done. Specific actions need to be taken before the actual training course starts. We link each action to one or more HILL building block(s) to indicate which building block is impacted by the action.

Action 1: Involvement of line manager

The line manager has the responsibility for guiding the overall learning processes of the employees and for supporting them in changing their behaviour. It is important to have a clear starting point and clearly defined objectives, otherwise the changes cannot be measured (Kessels, Smit, & Keursten, 1996; Pineda, 2014). Thus, the line manager needs to make sure what the starting situation and objectives of the employee are before the training starts. This implies that the line managers discuss with the employee what his or her current level of knowledge or skills is with regard to the topic of the training. The Academy can support line managers in this by sharing the core objectives of the training beforehand. Additionally, the employee can be stimulated to think about the desired level of knowledge or skills and what actions he or she will take to achieve this, alongside following the training. The Academy could provide a guidance procedure for this to the line managers to support them in this process. The procedure will include what topics to discuss and which questions to ask before and after participation in the training. This will facilitate the process of looking forward and will initiate goal setting, which will increase the chance of learning transfer taking place after the training has finished.

To even further enhance learning transfer, we would recommend cross-assigning line managers. In this way, the line managers are responsible for performance management and appraisals in their own department while being a coach for employees of another department. By doing this, the line managers will not feel constrained by conflicting responsibilities as a coach and as a line manager. Through these structured guidance procedures and cross-assignment of line managers the Academy can eliminate the conflicting responsibilities of a coaching line manager, which has a positive influence on building block 3 of the HILL approach: collaboration and coaching.

Action 2: Choose a 'support-giver'

To further enhance other forms of support-giving, another option would be to give employees the freedom to choose who they want to be supported by. If the choice of a support-giver is up to the employee, he or she can choose someone they feel comfortable with. An advantage of this possibility is that people are more open towards someone they feel at ease with. Therefore, the effects of coaching or other forms of support can be stronger. This process of choosing a support giver should be self-managed and initiated by the employee. However, the Academy can pave the way for this and ensure that everyone finds a coach or another support-giver, for instance by setting up an online discussion board or via the internal Wikipedia platform.

In general, if the connection between the support-giver and the employee is characterised as open, the quality of learning interactions is positively influenced. Consequently, the third HILL building block on collaboration and coaching will be impacted. As the initiative for this action lies with the employee, it also links to the second building block on self-management and learner agency.

Action 3: Learner community

As indicated in Chapter 3, most of the stakeholders at Scientor are aware of the importance of social interaction and cooperation at the workplace. Therefore, it would be interesting to increase cooperation throughout the whole learning process and enhance learning in a social context even further. As touched upon in the previous action, a learner community could facilitate more social interaction and collaboration between learners in the training programme. This community could encourage learners to share their ideas and knowledge with others. One way of doing this would be to provide an online discussion board that is accessible to the learners of a particular training programme. Here, learners could ask specific questions regarding that training and the discussion board would facilitate easy access to a social learning network. When learners are provided with the possibility to be part of a learner community and get in touch with others, the implementation of the third building block of the HILL model, Collaboration and Coaching, will be enhanced. Moreover, this action could facilitate a greater number of online and offline learning moments and increased knowledge sharing, which will improve the implementation of the HILL building blocks Hybrid Learning (block 4) as well as Action and Knowledge Sharing (block 5)

Action 4: Bring real-life examples

As stated earlier, learning needs are mostly identified on the job. The working environment offers an excellent opportunity to learn and should be incorporated into the training. More precisely, the Academy should ask participants to bring real-life cases and questions they encountered on the job to the training so as to discuss the issues at hand with their trainer and other learners. This way, learners identify new ways to combat problems and convert theory into practice immediately. Furthermore, these real-life examples can serve as a red thread throughout the training and deepen the understanding of the content matter at hand. By bringing real-life examples, the implementation of the building blocks Urgency, Gap, Problem (block 1) as well as Action and Knowledge Sharing (block 5) can be enhanced. By starting from real-life problems owned by the participants, you challenge participants and create urgency. Moreover, you stimulate and facilitate them to actively act upon these problems in close cooperation with colleagues, while sharing knowledge and insights on how to frame the issues encountered at work and how to work towards a solution.

Interventions during the training

There are several actions that can be initiated during the training in order to foster impactful learning. This phase describes the time from the beginning of a training course until its official end.

Action 1: Assign a co-learner

It is crucial to involve others in the learning process in order for the learning programme to achieve high impact; peers and colleagues are especially important (Hawley & Barnard, 2007; Pineda, 2014). Therefore, it is suggested to assign learners in a training programme to a co-learner who is following the same programme. The co-learners can assist each other in solving problems during and after the training or ask for information that they are lacking themselves. In this way, practical issues that might stand in the way of applying what has been learned into daily tasks can be more easily fixed. Thus, the Academy can facilitate and strengthen transfer of learning by assigning a co-learner for during and after training before the training officially starts. As a consequence, more social interaction and knowledge sharing will occur during and after training courses. The implementation of the building blocks Hybrid Learning (block 4), Collaboration and Coaching (block 3), and Action and Knowledge Sharing (block 5) are optimised by implementing this co-learner system.

Action 2: Define a plan for practical assignment/search online

In order to help the learner to apply in practice what he or she has learned during the training, a practical assignment to be completed in the weeks after the training can be co-developed with the learner. By co-developing, the assignment is tailored to the learner's specific job situation. The assignment can be part of a portfolio, for example, that provides a red thread from the phase before the training, to during and after the training. For instance, the final practical assignment for the after-training phase can look like a plan of action for a specific situation in the daily job of a learner, in which the content of the training can be applied and where the learner uses online sources for finding further information. By specifying concrete steps a learner wants to take and ensuring reflection questions are included in the assignment, transfer can be better guided and facilitated even after the learner leaves the classroom. The assignment can be sent to the trainer who will then provide feedback to give the learner an extra push to continue applying the lessons learned in his or her daily job. With this action, we fuel the learner's urgency to continue learning and his or her agency to take control of his or her own learning process and to keep on managing it. By stimulating the learner to go online for additional information, we enhance hybrid learning.

Action 3: Visual and electronic reminders and (e-)postcards

If a learner is reminded of a training course in the workplace, it will help them to transfer what was learned in this training (Pineda, 2010). For instance, before the end of a training programme, participants could write a postcard to themselves saying what they want to do differently when they return to the workplace. A month after the training, the first things a participant has learned during the training have become routines in the workplace. The Academy should make sure that the (e-)postcard the participant wrote to him- or herself is delivered to the participant within the first month after the training. This will help the participant to see whether the behaviour has changed as expected. Additionally, it will initiate a reflection moment, eventually in a chatgroup with colleagues. It triggers the employee to reconsider what was learned during the training. In this way, the learner reflects on the effect of the learning intervention and is reminded of the content of the training. This will increase the learning transfer. Another way to do this is by using visuals in the training. At the end of a training programme, similar visuals can be given or mailed to the learners so they could place these somewhere they could see them in their daily work. Hence, they would be reminded about the training in their daily job on a frequent basis. This action is initiated during the training and implemented after the training.

In line with action 2, this action, using online tools, stimulates learners to keep on engaging in learning and to self-monitor this continuous learning. In this way, this action facilitates the implementation of the building blocks Urgency, Gap, Problem; Learner Agency; and Hybrid Learning (blocks 1, 2 and 4).

Action 4: In-between reflection

Reflection and discussion moments should be inherent in the design of a training programme (Dochy, Berghmans, Koenen, & Segers, 2015). One example of how to put this into practice at Scientor is to include a specific reflection moment in the training. Halfway through the training, the trainer invites all learners to share what they have gained from the training so far and what they still want to learn in the second half. Thereby, learners can check and reflect on what they and others in the course have already learned. The Academy's role within this intervention is to ensure that such in-between reflection by the learners is actually guided by the trainers and is inherent to the initial training design. When learners are invited to share their learning moments together and give feedback to each other halfway throughout the training, the last building block, Assessment as Learning, as well as Action and Knowledge Sharing (block 7) will be better implemented at Scientor.

Interventions after the training

In order to realise impactful learning, activities initiated after a training course are highly important as well. There are several activities that can enable ongoing learning after the actual training course has finished.

Action 1: Update line manager

As touched upon in the before training phase, the involvement of line managers gives the participants a sense of support and could help with learning transfer. A manager could have a coaching role in which he or she helps the participant with his/her personal development, or a sponsor role in which the manager facilitates the learning activities of the participant (Cho & Egan, 2013). However, not all managers are aware of the role they have and therefore the Academy has to offer some help. For instance, it could be useful if the Academy provides questions after the training that the manager could pose to help the participant reflect on his or her learning process. This could help the participant to enrich his or her learning and to increase the learning impact. The Academy could send these questions a couple of weeks after the training to guide the line managers to assume their role in the learning process of the participant. Giving the line manager an active role in supporting learners to use the newly gained knowledge and skills, in reflection on what has been learned and how to use it, the building blocks of Collaboration and Coaching (block 3) as well as Assessment as Learning (block 7) are more optimally implemented at Scientor.

Action 2: Connect learner with experienced colleague

The involvement of a direct colleague as a buddy in the learning process of a learner can facilitate the application of knowledge. This should be a colleague who has more practical knowledge than the learner on the training topic. This person assists the learner in problem-solving, gives information that the learner lacks, and provides guidance. In addition to this, job-shadowing could be an option. This means that the learner could follow the experienced colleague around for a short amount of time. This way the learner could observe how the content of the training is applied in practice and he or she could imitate the new way of working. Afterwards he or she could apply it in his or her own daily job. Learning by imitation could help the learner to gain additional knowledge needed to apply the training lessons on the job. In this respect, the Academy can play a role in helping to connect learners with an experienced colleague. A digital platform can help employees in large organisations to find colleagues with the relevant experience.

By connecting to an experienced colleague, the building blocks Collaboration and Coaching (block 3) and Action and Knowledge Sharing (block 5) are implemented in a more optimal way than currently.

Action 3: Sharing lessons learned in a casual setting

Research shows that on average learners forget around 90% of what they have learned within the first month after a training course took place (Anderson, 2010). The Academy could mitigate this by stimulating people to share their lessons learned from a training course with others, and in this way increase the implementation of the building block Action and Knowledge Sharing (block 5). For example, this could be done in a casual setting in the learner's direct work environment and include team members, other colleagues, or the line manager. A casual setting such as having a coffee together or lunch can spark a conversation in which spontaneous learning can be facilitated. This will help to refresh the knowledge of the learner and spread the lessons learned to others as well. The chance of transfer of these lessons into practice will increase when more people are aware of the new knowledge. There are also many online opportunities to share lessons learned by adding, for example, blogs on the Scientor internal webpages or on the digital platform. In this way, hybrid learning is promoted.

Action 4: Follow-up meetings

Following up on a training course is helpful for the learners in order to reflect on how the application is going and being reminded of the content and lessons learned. The Academy could bring learners together after two to five months to discuss their experiences in applying what they have learned on the job. By then, the participants will be more aware of what they changed in their behaviour and can share their experiences to inspire and help others. Additionally, it provides an opportunity for feedback and reflection for themselves as well. This could give them a better understanding of how far they are into their learning process. All this will increase the learning impact. This is mostly applicable for skills that have multiple ways of being put into practice, such as soft skills. Technical skills will often have only one method of application and will therefore benefit less from face-to-face follow-up meetings. For technical training it might be more useful to provide a short Question & Answer moment in the first few weeks after the training. Specific issues learners encountered while using the technical skills can then be easily discussed and solved. This does not necessarily has to be a face-to-face meeting but could also be via e-mail or Skype.

When people take part in follow-up meetings, the building blocks Action and Knowledge Sharing (block 5) as well as Assessment as Learning (block 7) are more fully implemented.

Action 5: Apply plan and getting feedback (online)

Planning a practical assignment to use the newly acquired knowledge and skills in the weeks after the training (action 2, during the training) stimulates the learner to keep on learning. The plan can be read by another colleague to provide feedback (online or offline) as well as to give the learner an extra boost to continue applying the lessons learned in his or her daily job. The Academy plays an important role in monitoring whether plans are formulated and how the plans are executed by the learner and supported by the line manager. In this way, the learners are stimulated to keep on managing their learning process (building block 2: Learner Agency) and to learn from reflection and feedback on the application of what they have learned (building block 7: Assessment as Learning). By stimulating learners to make use of online opportunities and tools to provide feedback, hybrid learning is stimulated.

Moving further and beyond!

In the previous sections the focus was on short-term, hands-on actions that could be implemented rather quickly to reap the benefits from the HILL approach and to foster impactful learning. Moreover, a set of basic success factors was elaborated upon that were deemed value-adding due to the success of these short-term actions. In this section, we go one step further and look ahead to the future of the Academy (see Figure 6.4). Long-term recommendations are described to provide a first exploration of possible future activities the Academy could undertake. This is to further contribute to the strengths of the Academy. The themes discussed here are meant to be conversation-starters and a source of ideas for the long run; therefore, they are not necessarily described in full detail in this report.

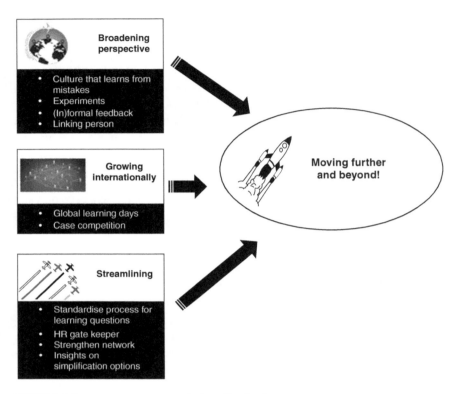

FIGURE 6.4 Long-term recommendations for the future

Broadening perspective

In order to keep up with the fast-changing business world, it is crucial to constantly question the world around us and look at things from different angles and in new ways. Only then is it possible to secure long-term success. By doing so, one can add more layers to the current mindset to make it more versatile. Therefore, we would recommend the Academy to broaden its perspective and spread it across the company so as to be able to deal with future challenges. The following four activities can help to extend the vision of the Academy and could further contribute to the success of implementing the HILL approach.

Action 1: Culture that learns from mistakes

The first step to broaden the perspective is establishing a culture that learns from – in contrast to solely accepts – mistakes. Thereby, it is important to actively recognise mistakes of employees in everyday tasks as something inevitable and good, as it provides an opportunity to learn and improve performance. The Academy can promote such a culture by providing tools that help managers and employees to establish it. For instance, searching for role models (managers or leaders that have already accepted the value of learning from mistakes) and letting them spread their beliefs and best practices throughout Scientor are relevant examples. Furthermore, the Academy can guide line and project managers in the initial phases of introducing such a culture. Many leaders are probably not used to the idea that mistakes provide extraordinary opportunities if they are detected and analysed in an effective way. More precisely, this means that the Academy should help leaders in going beyond a superficial assessment (e.g. 'rules were not followed') and instead getting to the bottom of the problem. Lastly, Scientor could benefit greatly from high-quality knowledge sharing between project teams all over the world to enhance its organisational learning. If the Academy can facilitate direct interaction between project teams to exchange lessons learned on mistakes, then it can also foster transfer of learning on an international and organisational level.

Action 2: Experiments

The next idea entails making room for experiments, learning moments and simply trying out new ideas. This would give employees the opportunity to dig deeper in projects and topics that they have a particular interest in. During the focus groups, one project leader gave a useful example of how he promotes this: every Friday afternoon his agenda is blocked to spend time on his own individual development. This principle could be extended to include individual interests and project experimentation as well. Even though it is not an easy task to make time available in very tightly organised projects, the efforts to do so would definitely help to broaden the view of the whole company. This is because experiments allow firms to learn, draw on new insights in very surprising ways, and boost innovation. The Academy should take an active role in facilitating this initiative by searching for best practices and ambassadors that would like to make it an organisational-wide flagship.

Action 3: (In)formal feedback

Feedback is traditionally viewed as a rather formal tool with which a supervisor or peer evaluates an individual's performance in a very structured manner. However, feedback could also be given more informally and spontaneously, for instance when having a coffee with a colleague or during an everyday chat with employees. People at Scientor are already partially making use of giving informal feedback. Nonetheless, we suggest placing a stronger focus on this concept and embedding it further in the company's culture. If feedback is understood as a wider concept in which it flows both formally and informally, performance gains and organisational goals can be reached quicker. The Academy should teach managers and employees how to give informal feedback and how to improve techniques of giving and receiving feedback. Thereby, the focus should lie on positive and constructive feedback. One example of giving quick informal feedback is advising managers to provide each of their employees with a suggestion of one thing to improve and one thing they did very well, on a monthly basis. This can easily be done in a very casual setting and does not need much time to prepare. This way, in the long run a culture that makes use of feedback will evolve naturally.

Action 4: Linking person

Furthermore, we recommend assigning someone who spreads the news and offerings of the Academy throughout the company. This person should take on a representative role and be the 'face of the Academy', whom employees can easily approach when they have questions or when they are generally interested in training opportunities. He or she would be responsible for all internal communication matters relevant to increasing the employees' awareness of the Academy. Hence, it might be advantageous to hire someone with a communication background. In a way, this person links the Academy to the rest of the organisation. The new wind that the person will blow through the Academy will also help to continuously come up with new solutions.

Growing internationally

In relation to the long-term recommendations on how to broaden the perspective of the Academy, it can also be recommended to expand the Academy's activities even further on an international scale. To lay a foundation for the global acknowledgement of the importance of the Academy's work, it would be helpful to let the Academy grow to the next level. Two practical activities the Academy could undertake to increase its international establishment within Scientor are described next. These will also positively influence the basic success factors discussed previously.

Action 1: Global learning days

The first activity the Academy could set up is an international Scientor Learning Day. On this day, the Scientor employees are able to experience different facets of learning through activities and workshops. To ensure global interest and involvement, the Scientor Learning Day could be hosted in every country at the same time. The Academy could coordinate with local HR managers to facilitate this day for their country. Additionally, it is a great opportunity for the Academy to invite external parties to promote learning and inspire the employees to become proactive learners. The Academy could invite inspirational speakers, researchers, learning scientists or other third parties who are connected to learning and can provide interesting and relevant workshops. The initiation of a Scientor Learning Day serves multiple purposes for the Academy, namely: it continues raising further awareness of the Academy itself and of the importance of learning. Further, it creates the opportunity to broaden the Academy's network on an international level, and it can lay the foundation for international acknowledgement of the value of the Academy's work in all layers of the organisation.

Action 2: International case competition

The second activity is based on a similar reasoning as the previous one for the Scientor Learning Day. This also has the purpose of putting the Academy on the international map throughout the whole organisation and increasing awareness of its added value. A creative way to enhance the positive image of the Academy even further and put the Academy in a new and different light is by organising international Case Competitions. These Case Competitions are for internal employees who can form international teams with colleagues from all over the world and compete with other teams to come up with the best solution to the case. The competition can also be hosted in a different country each year to foster involvement all over the globe. This leads to learning and working together in a fun, playful and international context. On the one hand, the cases can be based on struggles faced by the Academy or other Scientor departments. These can benefit from solutions and insights provided by other Scientor employees. The insights can be valuable because for some struggles it is necessary to know the company and its culture very well to be able to provide fitting solutions. On the other hand, cases can also be based on topics related to learning. Interesting issues that were discussed in training courses, for example, could serve as a basis for these cases.

Streamlining

When taking on new challenges such as broadening the Academy's perspective and growing internationally, it is important that the basis is already as strong as it can be. This means, for example, that the core activities and processes are streamlined so that no time is going to waste while executing these. Therefore, we would like to provide the Academy with some ideas on how to optimise their current activities and processes even further. These ideas are an extension of some of the basic success factors discussed previously.

Action 1: Standardise process for learning questions

Every day the Academy receives a substantial amount of learning questions that need to be collected and sorted out. According to the Academy's employees, this is a time-consuming activity, which is unfortunate because it takes time away from other important tasks. Therefore, it could be a solution to standardise this process as much as possible. Examples of how to do this include creating a database or a

Frequently Asked Questions page, on which people can first search for an answer on their learning question themselves before posing it to the Academy directly. Another idea could be to install something similar to a 'Customer Service chat'. This means that at certain times of the day there is a person available on this online chat who can help with learning questions on the spot. This person could provide an immediate answer to the simpler learning questions and allocate the more difficult questions to the right person.

Action 2: Reinforce HR's gatekeeping function

In addition to the previous suggestion, it could be useful to reinforce the gatekeeping function of HR with regard to learning questions. When HR managers officially have the responsibility to screen the learning questions first, and perhaps even categorise them for the Academy, it can relieve some of the Academy's workload. Moreover, it makes the process of collecting and sorting through the learning questions more structured and organised and therefore more streamlined. If the ties could become even stronger between the HR department and the Academy, there would be more clarity among themselves and towards others. Clarity is needed, for instance, on how to handle the large amount of learning questions, and additionally, on who has to provide the budget for what part of the Academy's activities. The strengthening of ties can be achieved through simple gestures such as dropping by at each other's office and having a cup of coffee.

Action 3: Strengthen your network

In general, it was noted by some learning consultants from the Academy that their work is often highly dependent on the willingness and availability of other people. Therefore, it would be recommendable for the Academy to ensure that its network is strong and vital, so that reciprocity becomes natural to everyone involved in this network. This sense of reciprocity can lead to people feeling more willing to make time for the learning consultants and help them to design proper training courses. Reciprocal behaviour has to come from both parties. However, one of them will have to initiate it and be a role model for the others.

Action 4: Get insights on simplification options

The suggestions made above can be of value to the Academy; however, it might be useful for the Academy to consider appointing a person who has more in-depth knowledge on streamlining processes and activities. This person could provide additional insights on more options for simplification that will relieve the employees of the Academy of some of the weight that is resting on their shoulders.

An overview of the basic success factors, and the short- and long-term recommendations with the golden principles as a foundation can be found in Figure 6.5.

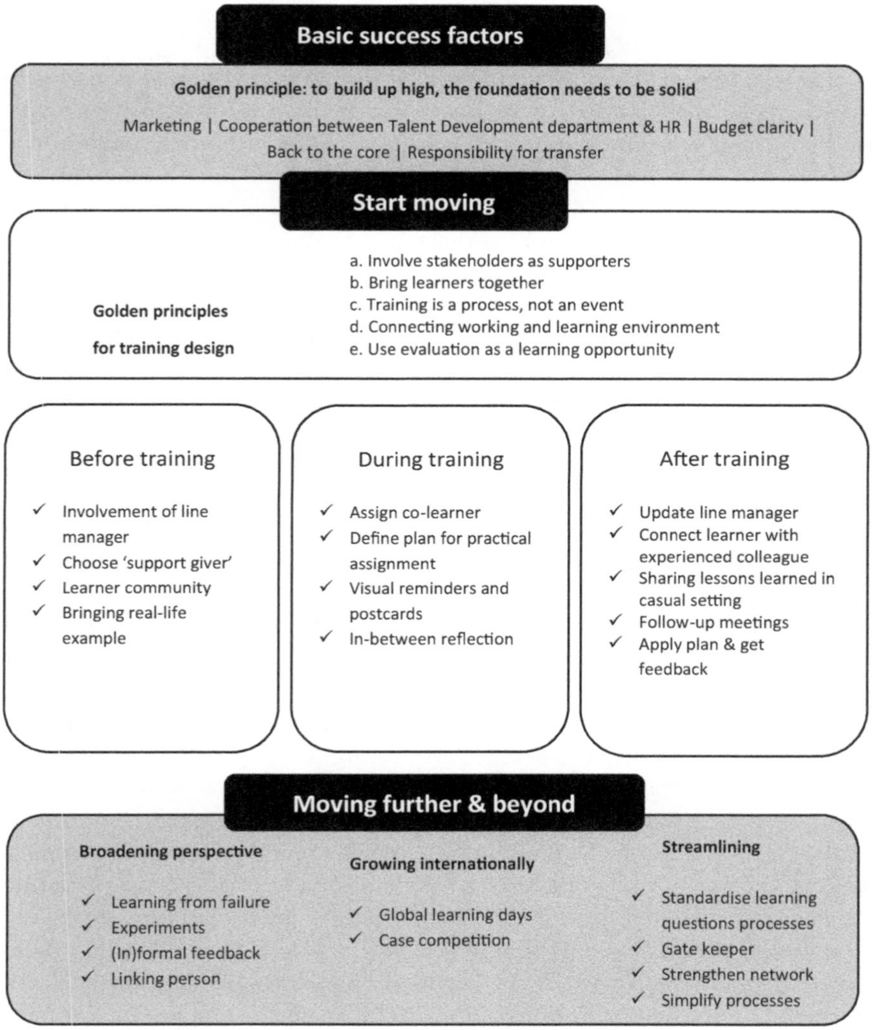

Basic success factors

Golden principle: to build up high, the foundation needs to be solid

Marketing | Cooperation between Talent Development department & HR | Budget clarity | Back to the core | Responsibility for transfer

Start moving

Golden principles

for training design

a. Involve stakeholders as supporters
b. Bring learners together
c. Training is a process, not an event
d. Connecting working and learning environment
e. Use evaluation as a learning opportunity

Before training

✓ Involvement of line manager
✓ Choose 'support giver'
✓ Learner community
✓ Bringing real-life example

During training

✓ Assign co-learner
✓ Define plan for practical assignment
✓ Visual reminders and postcards
✓ In-between reflection

After training

✓ Update line manager
✓ Connect learner with experienced colleague
✓ Sharing lessons learned in casual setting
✓ Follow-up meetings
✓ Apply plan & get feedback

Moving further & beyond

Broadening perspective

✓ Learning from failure
✓ Experiments
✓ (In)formal feedback
✓ Linking person

Growing internationally

✓ Global learning days
✓ Case competition

Streamlining

✓ Standardise learning questions processes
✓ Gate keeper
✓ Strengthen network
✓ Simplify processes

FIGURE 6.5 Overview of short- and long-term recommendations

3. Conclusion

In order to maintain Scientor's global market leader position, it is crucial to have a workforce that has up-to-date knowledge and skills. Part of the Academy's tasks is to facilitate high-quality training courses with a lasting effect. Therefore, it plays an important role in supporting Scientor's growth. The application of what is learned to the job is essential. In other words, impactful learning should be a high priority on the agenda of the Academy. To support the Academy, the HILL approach was used as a basis for this case analysis to answer the following question: *What actions can the Academy undertake to foster impact and transfer of learning, based on the High Impact Learning that Lasts (HILL) approach?*

The HILL approach offers a comprehensive overview of what is currently known about High Impact Learning and is therefore used as a basis to evaluate the current situation concerning High Impact Learning within Scientor. The evaluation of the current situation was used to build upon for the action plan. It was concluded that some of the HILL building blocks need more attention in the short term than others. Scientor had made some effort regarding a sense of urgency (block 1), learners' agency (block 2), and flexibility on formal and informal learning (block 6). Therefore, these building blocks need more attention in order to develop them further. We perceived that the other four building blocks currently have the most potential for growth and are virtually lacking. These are: Collaboration and Coaching (block 3), Hybrid Learning (block 4), Action and Knowledge Sharing (block 5), and Assessment as Learning (block 7).

In the action plan, our short-term recommendations focus on these four building blocks. In order to make the short-term actions even more effective, five basic success factors need to be worked on. These basic success factors include the marketing of the Academy, cooperation with the Talent Development department and the rest of the HR department, clarity on the allocation of the budget, a focus on the core activities of the Academy, and the responsibility for transfer of learning. The factors facilitate setting a focus, enhancing the integration and alignment with other departments, and raising awareness about the Academy. Moreover, having these factors in place strengthens the impact of the proposed short-term actions. The short-term recommendations called 'Start moving' are divided into three phases. Before the actual training, the Academy should initiate actions such as involving line managers and support givers, setting up a learner community and inviting learners to bring real-life examples to the training sessions. During the training, reflection moments and visual reminders should be incorporated and a co-learner could be assigned. After the training, recommended actions are to facilitate sharing knowledge within teams, and follow-up meetings. Additionally, the Academy could encourage the use of a practical post-training assignment. Lastly, line managers and direct colleagues should be involved again. If the Academy acts upon these recommendations, it benefits from a higher impact of the learning activities it provides. This relates to learners becoming more efficient and effective and the Academy gaining more control over the transfer process.

In addition to the short-term interventions, long-term recommendations have been formulated. These long-term recommendations are first ideas to initiate a conversation about possible future actions of the Academy. To broaden its perspective, it is suggested to establish a culture in which failure, experimenting, and both informal and formal feedback are included and used for learning. Additionally, the Academy could benefit from having a representative and linking person in their team. To facilitate international growth and awareness of the Academy, global Scientor Learning Days and Case Competitions could be organised. Lastly, to further streamline the Academy's processes it could standardise the

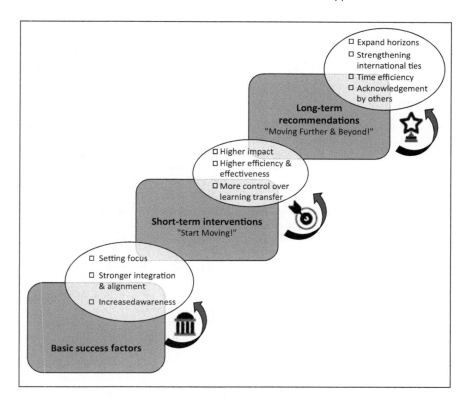

FIGURE 6.6 Overview of added value

learning questions process, improve the gatekeeping function of these questions, and strengthen its reciprocal network. In the long term, these recommendations could help to expand the Academy's horizons and improve its international ties. Additionally, the Academy will receive more acknowledgement of others and increase its time-efficiency.

The added value that the action plan offers to the Scientor Academy can be attained in three different stages, namely 'basic success factors', 'short-term interventions' and 'long-term recommendations'. As soon as the basic success factors are implemented, the Academy will benefit from a clear focus, stronger integration and alignment with other departments, as well as rising awareness within Scientor. This in turn gives a good foundation for implementing the short-term interventions. If these are rolled out successfully, they will result in higher learning impact, higher efficiency and effectiveness of the Academy's operations, as well as more control over the learning transfer. A solid basis can be expanded in the future by applying our long-term recommendations. They will help to expand the Academy's horizons, improve international ties, receive acknowledgement of others and increase time-efficiency as operations and processes are streamlined.

Note

1 Thanks to Pia Dworog, Kira Gendner, Inge Habermehl, Suvi Linna, Kim Mooren, Bas Roelofs and Selma Van der Haar for their input, data-gathering and reporting on this case.

Bibliography

Anderson, J. R. (2010). *Cognitive psychology and its implications.* New York, NY: Worth Publishing.

Appleby, M. (2013). Social learning. *Collector, 78*(10), 54–55.

Bartlett, K. R. (2001). The relationship between training and organizational commitment: A study in the healthcare field. *Human Resource Development Quarterly, 12*(4), 335–352.

Berghmans, I., Struyven, K., & Dochy, F. (2011). Door de ogen van de peer tutor. Een blik op de ervaren uitdagingen en factoren van invloed tijdens PAL [Through the eyes of a peer tutor: A look at the challenges and influencing factors during PAL]. *Tijdschrift voor Hoger Onderwijs [Journal for Higher Education], 29*, 257–270.

Bersin, J. (2006). Companies still struggle to tie training to business goals. *Training, 43*(10), 22–23.

Brookhart, S. M. (1999). Teaching about communicating assessment results and grading. *Educational Measurement: Issues and Practice, 18*(1), 5–13.

Cho, Y., & Egan, T. (2013). Organizational support for action learning in South Korean organizations. *Human Resource Development Quarterly, 24*(2), 185–213.

Dochy, F., & Nickmans, G. (2005). *Competentiegericht opleiden en toetsen. Theorie en praktijk van flexible leren* [Competence-based training and assessment: Theory and practice of flexible learning]. Utrecht, the Netherlands: Lemma.

Doornbos, A., Denessen, E., & Simons, R. (2004). *Leren van je werk. Verbanden tussen werkgerelateerde en individuele factoren in informeel leren bij de Nederlandse politie.* [Learning from work: Relations between work related and individual factors in informal learning in the Dutch police]. Utrecht, the Netherlands: ORD

Edmondson, A. (2012). *Teaming: How organizations learn, innovate, and compete in the knowledge economy.* Harvard, MA: Harvard Business School.

Govaerts, N., Kyndt, E., & Dochy, F. (2017). *Examining the effects of specific supervisor support types on transfer of training.* Paper presented at the EARLI conference, August, Tampere, Finland.

Hawley, J. D., & Barnard. J. (2007) Work environment characteristics and implications for training transfer: A case study of the nuclear power industry. *Human Resource Development International, 8*(1), 65–80.

Hoekstra, A., Brekelmans, M., Beijaard, D., & Korthagen, F. (2009). Experienced teachers' informal learning: Learning activities and changes in behavior and cognition. *Teaching and Teacher Education, 25*(5), 663–673.

Holton, E. F., Bates, R. A., & Ruona, W. E. A. (2000). Development of a generalized learning transfer system inventory. *Human Resource Development Quarterly, 11*(4), 333–360.

Kessels, J. W. M., Smit, K. A., & Keursten, P. (1996) Het achtvelden instrument: analyse kader voor opleidingseffecten [The instrument 'achtvelden': A frame for analysing effects of training]. Retrieved 23 April, 2015 from www.kessels-smit.nl/files/Het_acht_velden_instrument_NL_3.pdf

Martin, J. M. (2010). Workplace climate and peer support as determinants of training transfer. *Human Resource Development Quarterly, 21*(1), 87–104.

Marsick, V. J., & Volpe, M. (1999). The nature and need for informal learning. *Advances in Developing Human Resources, 1*(3), 1–9.

Pineda, P. (2010). Evaluation of training in organisations: A proposal for an integrated model. *Journal of European Industrial Training, 34*(7), 673–693.

Pineda, D. (2014). The feasibility of assessing teenagers' oral English language performance with a rubric. *Profile Issues in Teachers' Professional Development, 16*(1), 181–198.

Richter, D., Kunter, M., Klusmann, U., Lüdtke, O., & Baumert, J. (2011). Professional development across the teaching career: Teachers' uptake of formal and informal learning opportunities. *Teaching and Teacher Education, 27*(1), 116–126.

Roschelle, J., & Tasley, S. (1995). The construction of shared knowledge in collaborative problem solving. In C. E. O'Malley (Ed.), *Computer supported collaborative learning* (pp. 69–97). Heidelberg, Germany: Springer-Verlag.

Segers, M., & Tillema, H. (2011). How do Dutch secondary teachers and students conceive the purpose of assessment? *Studies in Educational Evaluation, 37*, 49–54.

Tough, A. (1971). *The adult's learning project: A fresh approach to theory and practice in adult learning.* Toronto, Canada: The Ontario Institute for Studies in Education.

Scientor N.V. (2015). *From company strategy to HR operations* [PowerPoint slides]. Retrieved from personal communication.

Van Roosmalen, G., Berghmans, I., Brants, L., Struyven, K., & Vierendeels, R. (2010). *Studenten leren van studenten. PAL inspiratiegids* [Students learn from students: PAL inspirational guide]. Geel, Belgium: Capina Media.

Vaughan, K., & Cameron, M. (2009). *Assessment of learning in the workplace: A background paper (Research Report No. 1).* Retrieved from Industry Training Federation Research Network website: https://akoaotearoa.ac.nz/download/ng/file/group-1656/n3143-assessment-of-learning-in-the-workplace-a-background-paper.pdf

CASE 2: HOW TO SUPPORT LIFELONG LEARNING THAT IS ON-DEMAND AND JUST-IN-TIME?

A CASE FROM THE TECHNOLOGY SECTOR[1]

EXECUTIVE SUMMARY

This case report contributes to Smart Industry's Action Agenda by offering a theoretical framework on how on-demand and just-in-time lifelong learning trajectories should be developed, as well as recommendations on how practice should move forward to be able to develop such high-impact trajectories. In order to do so, we reviewed relevant literature and interviewed managers of educational institutions with responsibility for providing lifelong learning pro-grammes, so-called Centres of Expertise. In addition to this, experts in the field of learning in the technology sector were interviewed.

The main motive for this case analysis was the notion that the current learn-ing approach has to change in order to maintain a leading position in the technology sector. As the technology sector is like any other sector, chang-ing fast, it is necessary to keep human capital up-to-date through lifelong learning. However, the current learning approach focuses on very traditional approaches to learning, such as a too strong emphasis on teaching content to learners, and therefore does not comply with the need for lifelong learning initiatives. In order to ensure that education fits into professionals' busy lives, lifelong learning trajectories should be on-demand and just-in-time. Moreover, the trajectories should foster HILL to ensure effective learning which can be transferred into the field of practice. ICT-related learning tools play a key role in the development of such trajectories. Not only do they allow for learning at any time and any place, they may also contribute to implementing High Impact Learning since an electronic or physical environment may force trainers and coaches to work in ways that are less dictated by longstanding habits.

The development of on-demand and just-in-time HILL/lifelong learning initiatives imposes several challenges. For example, how should such learning trajectories be structured? What kind of ICT-related learning tools fit best in this structure? Furthermore, questions can be asked as to what the role of the trainer should be in lifelong learning trajectories supported by ICT-related learning tools.

We created a model that combines these different factors (structure, tools, trainer), as they reinforce each other. The model implies that the structure of a learning trajectory can be divided into several phases. To create a fitting learning path, every learning trajectory should start with a pre-assessment of the individual's current knowledge. Then, to effectively acquire knowledge, we propose the use of ICT-related learning tools that inspire high impactful learning that lasts while also promoting on-demand and just-in-time learning. To effectively apply knowledge, we propose that face-to-face contact is most beneficial. Hereby, we advise that the learner has face-to-face contact with a coach and practises with actual tools. To foster HILL and thus increase hybridity, we recommend the inclusion of interaction possibilities with both peers and a coach throughout the entire learning trajectory. The moment the individual is satisfied with his or her learning process, he or she should be able to keep in contact with the coach to receive support after the official learning trajectory has ended.

Fitting to the structure and the use of ICT-related learning tools, we propose that the trainer should function more as a coach throughout the learning trajectory. This is done by, for example, building a trustful relationship, discussing learning goals, providing feedback and guiding the learner. Working with learning management tools implies that the instructor should have at least a basic level of technological knowledge. However, the biggest challenge for instructors may be to change their mindset. They have to recognise that they cannot be all-knowing at all times. Working with professionals in a vastly changing technology sector implies that instructors may have to look for additional sources to find the required knowledge material. Nevertheless, as we found that interaction fosters High Impact Learning that Lasts, the instructor will still play a key role by guiding and supporting individuals in their learning process to increase hybridity.

It is hoped that this will inspire those responsible for providing programmes to facilitate lifelong learning to look for optimal solutions to make individual, on-demand and just-in-time lifelong learning possible.

1. Introduction: Industry 4.0 and cyber-physical systems

Over the last three centuries, three industrial revolutions had a significant impact on our society. These three industrial revolutions were a result of standardisation, automation, the introduction of electricity and the use of electronics and IT. As the industry of technology keeps on developing, Europe is currently in the middle of a fourth industrial revolution. This revolution was first made public knowledge at the Hannover Messe 2012 in Germany. This fourth revolution, also referred to as 'Industry 4.0', is a result of the evolution of PCs into smart devices and the interconnectivity between smart devices through the internet. This change results in a merge of the physical world and the virtual world in the form of Cyber-Physical Systems (CPSs). CPSs are integrations of computation with physical processes, where networks monitor and control the physical processes (Lee, 2008). Examples of these CPSs are storage systems and production facilities that are capable of autonomously exchanging information. By making use of these CPSs, it is now possible to network resources, information, objects and people to create the Internet of Things and Services. The Internet of Things and Services results in the possibility to create networks that incorporate the complete manufacturing process and in this way convert factories into smart factories. This technological evolution of CPSs will be felt by the manufacturing industries and is therefore described as Industry 4.0.

Industry 4.0 is focusing on creating smart products, procedures and processes, in which smart factories are a key feature. Humans, machines and resources are working together in smart factories. Resulting from this collaboration, smart factories are able to manufacture goods more efficiently and to manage complex situations. Its interactions with smart mobility, smart logistics and smart grids will make a smart factory the key component of tomorrow's smart infrastructures. These components combined, and the increasing use of the Internet of Things and Services in manufacturing, will transform conventional value chains and will lead to the emergence of new business models (Kagermann, Wahlster, & Helbig, 2013). An overview of what Industry 4.0 looks like and how it is cooperating with other key areas is presented in Figure 6.7.

Because of the evolution and changes within the manufacturing industry, Industry 4.0 provides huge potential. Smart factories allow for manufacturing processes to meet individual customer demands while still being profitable (Kagermann et al., 2013). Similarly, the usage of smart technologies allows for diverse and flexible career paths. Flexible career paths allow people to work productively for longer periods of time (Kagermann et al., 2013). This is especially important in light of changing demographics and policy responses across the European continent (European Commission, 2016). These examples of the potential benefits of Industry 4.0 suggest that the manufacturing industry has some promising potential and might have a bright future.

Nevertheless, the road towards Industry 4.0 highlights some challenges that must be overcome. Programme developers identified several challenges that might

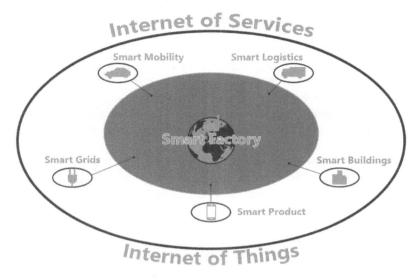

FIGURE 6.7 Industry 4.0 and smart factories as part of the Internet of Things and Services (Kagermann et al., 2013)

hinder successful implementation of Industry 4.0. These include standardisation issues, product availability and work organisation (Kagermann et al., 2013). Once these challenges are overcome, Industry 4.0 will have an impact on the global competitiveness of sectors and the manufacturing industry in general.

Following the development and implementation of Industry 4.0 in Germany, several other European countries created development programmes in order to improve or maintain their positions in the field of technology. For example, Manufacturing Catapult was created in the UK and Factory of the Future in Italy and France. Similarly, Smart Industry was created in the Netherlands.

2. Industry 4.0 asks for a different approach to learning

Industry 4.0 challenges our current L&D policies and practices. In order to innovate, one needs access to the right kind of knowledge at the right time. As the technology sector is changing at a rapid pace, the knowledge of graduates in the sector becomes (as in any sector) obsolete in relatively short periods of time (De Grip & Van Loo, 2002). This so-called 'half life time of knowledge' increases the need for lifelong learning for employees (Gerards, De Grip, Hoon, Kühn-Nelen, & Poulissen, 2015). It is thus of great importance that graduates working in industry invest in learning throughout their career path. Learning can keep their knowledge up-to-date and relevant, adapted to new developments, new operating systems, new software and apps, which is not only of great value for the individual, but also for the company and society. Having up-to-date and relevant knowledge increases the employability of the employee (Thijssen, Van der Heijden, & Rocco, 2008).

However, currently, employees are often not able to find the right knowledge at the right time in order to update their knowledge in a relevant and timely fashion. The existing learning approach focuses mostly on frontal learning: educational classes, group courses and group training, all focused on teaching similar content to learners. This learning approach assumes that these individuals all have the same level of pre-knowledge and are all interested in learning the same subject and materials (Benigno & Trentin, 2000).

However, tomorrow's business is characterised by its high level of dynamism and a large variety in discipline specialisations. A result of this dynamism is that individuals are wanting to acquire different knowledge or skills at different times. Therefore, maintaining a top position asks for a different learning approach that focuses on individual lifelong learning, which is on-demand and just-in-time. This can offer employees the opportunity to find the right knowledge at the right time and consequently support innovation (Chesbrough, Vanhaverbeke, & West, 2014; Drucker, 2014; Roco & Bainbridge, 2013). The use of hybrid learning tools can support such a learning approach, as it allows individuals to seek learning materials at any time and any place (Hirsch & Ng, 2011; Rubens, Kaplan, & Okamoto, 2012; Russell et al., 2013). Although there is a vast amount of learning materials available online, there is a lack of learning support that motivates employees to finish the online learning process they have started and that supports the application of what is learned into their work (Siemens, 2013). This raises several questions as to how a learning approach can support individual, on-demand and just-in-time lifelong learning.

The concept of lifelong learning can only reach its maximal impact when it is mutually reinforced by three key players: educational institutions, businesses and the government. The more these three key stakeholders reinforce each other, the greater the chance that lifelong learning initiatives will become successful. Creating a fitting infrastructure for learning professionals can function as the first step in the development of successful lifelong learning trajectories. However, one should not forget that this infrastructure will only succeed when it is supported by all stakeholders: businesses, the government, and professional training institutes.

2.1 What is lifelong learning?

The concept of lifelong learning can be described as 'learning that is pursued throughout life: learning that is flexible, diverse and available at different times and in different places' (Srebrenkoska, Mitrev, Atanasova-Pacemska, & Karov, 2014). In other words, lifelong learning implies that learning takes place before and after, as well as during, traditional education (e.g. primary school, high school, university etc.). The learners themselves are responsible for their own learning trajectory and can choose themselves to what extent they want to pursue learning. Through lifelong learning, individuals can improve, update and complement their current knowledge over time.

2.2 On-demand and just-in-time learning

Contrary to traditional learning, which is characterised by group learning in formal classes, lifelong learning asks for a different learning approach. Professionals in the work field who need or wish to learn more after their formal education often do not have the time and/or other resources to participate in formal traditional learning programmes. Often, professionals also wish to learn specific parts of learning materials instead of completing an entire learning trajectory. Moreover, professionals can differ in the degree of difficulty in knowledge or skills they wish to obtain due to varying levels of pre-knowledge. For these reasons, professionals who wish to broaden their knowledge or skills should be able to learn what they want at any time and any place. In other words, a learning approach supporting lifelong learning should be focused on the individual and should be on-demand and just-in-time in order to be practical (Broek & Buiskool, 2012; Jaspers & Heijmen-Versteegen, 2004). In this respect, technology nowadays offers many possibilities to learn on-demand and just-in-time. By investing in technology, providers of lifelong learning programmes can foster hybrid learning, a well-thought-out combination of online and offline learning.

2.3 Interconnection between education and business

In order to support lifelong learning, several other factors, besides the learning content and the difficulty of the content being individualised, available on-demand and just-in-time, are deemed necessary. One of the most important factors is the interconnection between business and educational institutions. Educational institutions can function as the providers of knowledge that professionals need for their lifelong learning. However, the integration of business and education has multiple ways of supporting the development of a skilled workforce in the technology sector.

(1) By making educational institutions and businesses more intertwined, both can benefit from each other's knowledge, resources and facilities. This is beneficial from a business perspective, as employees can make use of the wide variety of materials and machines that technically oriented educational institutions usually possess. From an educational perspective, businesses may influence professionals in starting their learning trajectory.
(2) Businesses can contribute to the education of both regular students and professionals. More specifically, by becoming more connected to educational institutions, businesses create an opportunity to influence the learning materials and content to promote the inclusion of the most relevant and innovative knowledge from their field of expertise.

TABLE 6.1

Key takeaways

The need for lifelong learning has become undeniable, due to rapidly changing knowledge in the technology sector.

Lifelong learning should be individual, on-demand and just-in-time in order to be practical; this implies investment in hybrid learning.

Interconnection between educational institutions and business supports movement of lifelong learning.

---

(3) Businesses gain more insight into the workforce of the future. This allows them to select only those people they consider to have the most suitable knowledge and the highest learning potential. In addition, students will be able to obtain a more accurate impression of what specific job descriptions will look like.

3. Challenges for Smart Industry

The main goal of this case analysis is to provide insights into how to support on-demand and just-in-time lifelong learning among professionals. The main question of this case analysis is therefore as follows:

> *How can you support individual, on-demand and just-in-time lifelong learning that is supported by hybrid tools?*

In addition:

- What should the structure of hybrid learning trajectories that support on-demand and just-in-time lifelong learning look like?
- What hybrid tools are available to support this structure?
- How does the role of the instructor change when shifting from a 'teaching' approach to a HILL approach?

In this case analysis, we focus on educational institutions with responsibilities for offering professional lifelong learning programmes. In the Netherlands, they are referred to as Centres of Excellence.

4. How to realise lifelong learning trajectories that foster High Impact Learning?

When focusing on the development of lifelong learning initiatives, there are several factors related to learning that will have to change to support individual, on-demand and just-in-time learning. These are the structure of learning trajectories, the use of ICT-related learning tools and the role of the instructor.

4.1 Structure of learning trajectories

As described previously, learning trajectories need a structure that allows for the inclusion and development of elements that increase High Impact Learning while at the same time adhering to the requirements of lifelong learning. In this section, we discuss how face-to-face and ICT-related learning can be best combined while at the same time allowing learners to step in with different levels of pre-knowledge.

4.1.1 How to combine online and offline learning?

Lee (2010) conceptualised a model that focuses on a structure that can be used as an example of how to best integrate online and offline learning (see Figure 6.8). The model makes a distinction between the available learning paths: online knowledge acquisition and offline performance capacity-building. Hereby, two implications underline the model. First, learning should occur through the use of cases and problems in order to be work-based. Second, the different learning phases imply different learning activities and different roles for the instructor (for a broader discussion, see '4.3 The role of the instructor').

The first phase is online knowledge acquisition, which implies acquiring knowledge (activation phase) and acquiring knowledge for use (demonstration phase) (Holton & Baldwin, 2003). In the activation phase, learning activities are promoted when relevant previous experience is activated ('know that'). In the demonstration phase, learning activities are promoted when the instructor demonstrates what is to be learned ('know how') (Merrill, 2002). This first phase emphasises interaction, which refers to the learner–learner contact and learner–instructor contact that needs to foster hybridity.

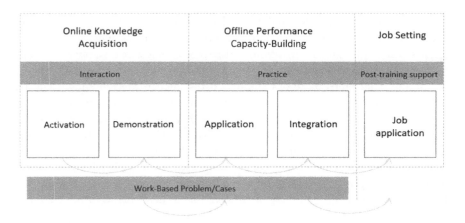

FIGURE 6.8 A distinction between learning phases and recommended learning steps (Lee, 2010)

The second phase, offline performance capacity-building, consists of building performance capacity through practice (application phase) and application for job-specific proficiency (integration phase).

In the application phase, learning is promoted when learners are required to use their new knowledge or skills to solve problems. In the integration phase, learning is promoted when learners are encouraged to integrate (transfer) knowledge into their everyday life (Merrill, 2002). In this phase, whether someone learns all depends on real-life practice.

Finally, in the job setting phase, people learn by repeating and maintaining application throughout their daily job. Based on the learning activities in each of these phases, the combination of online and offline learning activities, as proposed here, may provide a structure for the design of effective learning trajectories.

4.1.2 Different levels of pre-knowledge

When focusing on individual, on-demand and just-in-time lifelong learning, one can imagine that not every learner wishes to acquire the exact same content. Moreover, there may also be significant differences in learners' pre-knowledge of a given subject. Each learner has a distinct level of pre-knowledge. While some learners might wish to start with the basics of understanding, others might already have had some practice and are rather looking to enable an advanced skill set. This has implications for the structure of lifelong learning trajectories, as it requires that learners should be able to jump in at different levels. Bloom's taxonomy (1965) gives insights into how different learning levels are developed. Bloom's taxonomy of the cognitive domain is a classification in which different learning objectives are distinguished. The first stage, 'remember', implies recalling facts, terms, basic concepts and answers. The second stage, 'understand', goes one step further and implies that information can be structured, organised and interpreted. In the third stage, 'apply', the learner should be able to use the learned knowledge to solve new problems. In the fourth stage, one can distinguish between three stages: 'analyse, evaluate and create'. In analysing, connections are made among ideas, whereas evaluating implies critically judging information. Furthermore, being able to apply knowledge enables learners to also create something new from the built knowledge.

An important prerequisite of the model is that higher levels of knowledge can only be reached when lower levels are already obtained. The taxonomy implies that knowledge can only be understood when it is remembered, that knowledge can only be applied when it is understood, and that knowledge can only be analysed, evaluated and/or used to create something new when it can be applied.

However, Bloom's taxonomy is not without controversy. Dochy, Berghmans, Koenen, and Segers (2015) proclaim that a learning process is not a linear process. Rather, learning involves an integral crossover of all the elements of the cognitive domain. However, given the requirements of individual lifelong learning, the taxonomy still remains of added value. It can function as a base for the design of lifelong learning trajectories. Similarly, it indicates that different tools and support are applicable in different learning processes. Also, as different levels in knowledge exist, instructors need to know which level of knowledge an individual learner currently has. Bloom's taxonomy provides a framework for classifying the individual's level of knowledge and adapting learning trajectories accordingly.

To deal with variation in the pre-knowledge of learners, instructors in cooperation with learners need to analyse individuals' pre-knowledge and learning needs. Lee's trajectory (Figure 6.8) offers a valid framework to ascertain the learners' level of proficiency. By offering evidence on learning activities undertaken in the past and past work performance, the learner can make transparent which phase of the learning trajectory is the right starting point for him or her. It is the role of the instructor to guide the learner in this self-assessment process and to take a decision together with the learner on where to start the learning trajectory.

What should the structure of learning trajectories that support individual, on-demand and just-in-time lifelong learning look like?

Although the usage of ICT-related learning tools offers distinct benefits, we propose that learning trajectories should be hybrid, and thus include face-to-face learning as well. A combination of both (hybrid learning) is found to foster HILL the most. In particular, these tools can support learning in different phases. While ICT-related learning tools can be easily used when acquiring knowledge, face-to-face content is proposed for the application of knowledge. As individuals should be able to step in at any learning phase, the trajectory should start with assessing the individual's level of current knowledge. Subsequently, appropriate learning trajectories, including the right learning phases, can be designed. This design should focus on the inclusion of interaction possibilities at all times, as this proposed interaction fosters HILL. Furthermore, the structure can enhance High Impact Learning by making the learning process active, flexible and self-manageable by the learners while instructors provide work-based problems in all phases.

Key takeaways
- *The four phases of a learning trajectory (activation, demonstration, application and integration) offer a structure for defining the balance between online and offline learning activities.*
- *Different levels of prior knowledge ask for different starting points in the learning trajectory.*

4.2 ICT-related hybrid learning tools

In the previous section, we discussed the structure of the learning trajectory regarding individual, on–demand and just-in-time lifelong learning in the context of

HILL. Following the structure that combines online and offline learning, the need for ICT-related learning tools became clear. It is therefore important to investigate the different kinds of ICT-related learning tools to see how these tools can contribute and can fit in the structure of hybrid learning trajectories. Below, we examine currently used and newly developed ICT-related learning tools and classify them according to their main differences. Furthermore, we relate them to the HILL model to identify when a certain tool can be best used.

4.2.1 Types of ICT-related learning tools

Overall, ICT-related learning tools can be divided into four broad categories. We will look into each separate category and describe what it entails and why the included tools are different from the others. Nevertheless, it should be recognised that the field of ICT-related learning tools is booming and the list only gives a few out of many existing examples that are popular and well developed.

Knowledge transfer tools

The ICT-related learning tools belonging to this category solely focus on the transfer of knowledge from instructor to participant. Although these tools can be used in a broader framework which includes interaction, there is typically no interaction between instructors and participants while using these tools. Tools focusing on the transfer of specific knowledge can be prepared by the instructors themselves or can be obtained from another source. Examples of knowledge transfer tools are:

- *Blog*: A single or multiple text(s) containing specific knowledge.
- *Vlog*: A single or multiple video(s) containing specific knowledge.
- *Podcast*: An audio set containing specific knowledge.

Classroom connectors

This type of tool focuses on the recreation of a classroom: participants can find information and engage with instructors as well as other participants. In other words, participants are provided with the learning tools while their questions and discussions are monitored by knowledgeable instructors. It often contains online classrooms, forums and multimedia content.

- *Blackboard:* Blackboard is a platform in which instructors can post information and content while participants can post questions to the instructors and engage with other participants. It allows for individual learning as well as peer learning through a variety of tools used to represent a classroom.
- *Wallwisher:* Participants can build virtual classroom 'Walls', in which they can post 160-character messages containing web links, images, videos and audio.

Besides keeping notes, it also allows for collaborative activities. Before participants can contribute, instructors have to approve the content.

Collaboration platforms

The tools belonging to this category focus solely on the sharing and collaboration between participants. These tools often do not include instructors' participation. They allow participants to share their knowledge, correct each other's mistakes and contribute to each other's knowledge.

* *GoogleDoc*: Participants can write down content on an online page. Simultaneously, other permitted participants can add content or change the written content. Comments can be placed for explanation What is written, corrected or commented on by others is marked up.
* *Wiki*: Similar to GoogleDoc, Wiki allows for collaborative modification of its structure and content directly from the web. It results in a text containing the collaborative knowledge of its participants.

Interactive learning environments

A new development in the world of ICT-related learning tools is the development of Interactive Learning Environments (for more information on the development, see section 4.2.2 on artificial intelligence). An Interactive Learning Environment (ILE) can be described as an IT-based learning environment, which is interactive in nature (Renkl & Atkinson, 2007). In this case, interactive refers to mutual dependence of the learners' actions and the learning environment they are in (Renkl & Atkinson, 2007; Wagner, 1994). More specifically, learners have the opportunity to actively work with the learning material rather than solely taking in presented information. What is learned is therefore dependent on their learning behaviour in ILEs. Next, we describe two examples:

* *Intelligent tutoring systems*: Intelligent tutoring systems (ITSs) are computerised learning environments that include the presence of an artificial intelligence tutor. The artificial intelligence tutor can track the learner's degree of knowledge, skills, motivation, strategies and even emotions (Graesser, Conley, & Olney, 2012). It can provide answers, comments and feedback that best support the individual learning process. There are multiple kinds of ITSs, which focus on different knowledge and/or skills that should be learned.
* *Virtual world*: A virtual world may be described as an online, computer-based program that mimics the real world. By using their virtual representation (avatars), people can communicate and cooperate with each other, mimicking the real world (Liu, Zhong, Ozercan, & Zhu, 2013). Virtual worlds can include ITSs, so artificial intelligence tutors can provide learning guidance in the virtual world.

MOOCs: Massive Online Open Courses

Although a MOOC is often incorrectly referred to as a learning tool, it is rather a combination of tool(s) that together form a trajectory. MOOC stands for Massive Online Open Course and is available to everybody who desires to participate (Margaryan, Bianco, & Littlejohn, 2015). The creators of MOOCs are free to design the structure and to choose what kind of learning tools as well as assessment tools are included. Below, we describe the two most popular types of MOOCs (Lane, 2012; Margaryan et al., 2015; Smith & Eng, 2013):

- *xMOOC:* A content-based MOOC which is characterised by the lecture model. Instructors often offer students content through video lectures after which they formulate a final (online) exam. In an xMOOC, the content is prepared by the instructor and the assessments are computer-marked. During the MOOC, there is no interaction between the instructor and the participant. In other words, participants learn solely through the transmission of knowledge from the instructor to the participant via the use of the internet. The xMOOC has been the most popular type of MOOC so far. Starting rates are high and dropout rates are also very high (mostly around 95%).
- *cMOOC:* A network-based MOOC characterised by connectivity learning (Siemens, 2005). Participants formulate their own learning goals and try to reach these together with their fellow students. Instructors support students by taking on the role of a coach. In a cMOOC, the learning materials are open for editing. Thus, cMOOCs are characterised by the *autonomy of the learner* as there is no formal curriculum, *diversity* as the tools and content vary, *interactivity* as knowledge emerges from communication, and *openness* as it is accessible to everyone (Downes, 2014). As a result, there is no formal assessment and participants decide whether what is learned is sufficient for them.

Overall, which type of MOOC is referred to depends on the learning type (Lane, 2012; Siemens, 2005). The type of learning is fostered by the type of ICT-related learning tools that are included in the learning trajectory. For example, using knowledge transfer tools which are not interactive is characteristic of xMOOCs and the lecture model. On the other hand, tools that are highly interactive are more characteristic of cMOOCs and connectivity learning (Lane, 2012; Siemens, 2005).

4.2.2 Artificial intelligence and learning

The development of educational resources is moving towards a new field. Instead of traditional sources (such as lectures, books and classrooms), Interactive Learning Environments take what is best from traditional sources (mainly one-on-one tutoring) and combine it with ICT-related tools (Graesser et al., 2012; Liu et al., 2013). The creators of Interactive Learning Environments believe that artificial intelligence tutors can better guide students' learning as they are better able to adapt to student needs. As opposed to human tutors, artificial intelligence tutors do not base their teaching strategy on expectations they have of their students (Graesser et al., 2012).

Intelligent tutoring systems have shown to greatly contribute to the learning of individuals: a study has shown that students who received teaching from intelligent tutoring systems outperformed students who received only traditional teaching in 92% of the cases (Kulik & Fletcher, 2016).

4.2.3 Classification of ICT-related learning tools

As discussed above, ICT-related learning tools are shifting in their levels of interactivity and the level of support that is given by the instructor. A visualisation of how the categories are related to one another is presented in the box below. The first ICT-related learning tools such as online lectures and videos (knowledge transfer tools) do not allow for any communication and any support from the instructor, while new developments (Interactive Learning Environments) are designed around communication and support possibilities.

According to the HILL model, interaction between peers and support from a coach is necessary for impactful learning that lasts. Therefore, one would assume that it is best to use tools that allow for high interactivity and high levels of instructor support. However, this may depend on the learning structure in which the tool will be used. For example, in the context of the HILL model, courses that are 100% online (such as MOOCs) are recommended to include ICT-related learning tools that allow for high levels of interactivity and the strong support of a coach (Dochy et al., 2015) to increase hybridity. On the other hand, creators of trajectories that are only 50% online may opt for more offline interactivity and may therefore require less online interactivity. Overall, the ICT-related tools should contribute to the structure of the learning trajectories to complement its High Impact Learning factors while supporting individual, on-demand and just-in-time lifelong learning.

What ICT-related tools are available to support this structure? Which ones should be used?

As mentioned previously, ICT-related learning tools are indispensable in lifelong learning trajectories that are individual, on-demand and just-in-time. Furthermore, they can contribute to HILL. However, they only contribute to impactful learning when they allow for a sufficient level of interaction between peers and between the learner and the instructor. We have identified four types of ICT-related learning tools so far: Knowledge Transfer Tools, Classroom Connectors, Collaboration Tools and Interactive Learning Environments. The most promising tools are those that score high on interaction possibilities between peers and between the learner and a coach: tools belonging to the category of Interactive Learning Environments. However, it has to be kept in mind that the most useful tool may depend on the other factors as well (i.e. learning content and learning context). Moreover, in order to fully leverage the benefits that these tools provide, they have to be fully embedded within the structure of the learning trajectory; ICT-learning tools should contribute to active learning as opposed to passive learning.

In practice, we see that the tools that are currently mostly used do not allow for high levels of interaction. Rather, the most often-used tools can be classified as 'knowledge transfer tools', which score the lowest on interaction possibilities. Therefore, we recommend L&D programme providers to also focus on other possibilities related to ICT-related learning tools. Although Interactive Learning Environment tools adapted for different subjects may not be available to the masses yet, it is advised that centres should look for tools that allow for higher levels of interaction between peers as well as between learners and the instructor.

Key takeaways:
- **There are different types of ICT-related learning tools, which differ in their degree of peer interaction and instructor support.**
- **The tools should inspire High Impact Learning.**
- **Which tool is best to use depends on what the learning structure looks like.**

4.3 The role of the instructor

How does the role of the instructor change when shifting from group learning to individual learning?

The most fundamental change regarding the context of the role of the instructor in such new learning trajectories may be the increased self-ownership and activity of the learner. Individuals now self-construct their knowledge, which is transferred through the use of ICT-related learning tools as opposed to the traditional instructor. However, both active and hybrid learning asks for the support of a coach. The instructor should therefore not focus on the transfer of knowledge, but focus more on supporting, guiding, providing feedback and assessing the student in a way that fits his or her individual learning trajectory. This is related to both knowledge acquisition phases as well as knowledge application phases; however, this applies especially in the knowledge application phase due to the required face-to-face contact. Furthermore, instructors of individual, on-demand and just-in-time learning trajectories should not only have subject- or domain-specific expertise but also a sufficient level of technological knowledge and skills in order to work with ICT-related learning tools.

Insights from practice in the Centres of Expertise show us that not every instructor currently performs tasks that are related to being a coach. Furthermore, there were indications of resistance among instructors to work with ICT-related learning tools and to take on the supporting role of a coach. Similarly, we noticed that centres are wondering how they should inspire the development of becoming coaches among their instructors. Therefore, we recommend centres to develop instructor profiles that describe the roles, activities and competences of instructors that can support learning trajectories as we propose. This can then be used in recruitment processes as well as performance management processes to ensure that the instructor is contributing to HILL in the individual, on-demand and just-in-time lifelong learning trajectories.

4.4 Our framework for lifelong learning trajectories that inspires High Impact Learning that Lasts

In the model below, we combined all of our findings into one overall framework. It can function as inspiration and a blueprint for the development of future individual, on-demand and just-in-time learning trajectories. As discussed previously, this model includes the structure of the learning course including focus points, the different tools that can be used and the role of the instructor. In general, learners start in a pre-learning phase and end in a post-learning phase. However, we would like to emphasise that within the context of lifelong learning, individuals will switch between the different phases and go back and forth. In the context of lifelong learning, individuals might want to update knowledge, complement their knowledge and/or brush up already existing knowledge continuously. In other words, the learning trajectories should not be characterised by a linear learning process. Rather, learners should be able to jump in at any level and move back and forth through the different phases in a way that best fits their learning needs.

4.4.1 Activities that complement our framework

In each of these learning phases as proposed in Figure 6.8, specific activities should be performed that are coherent with the HILL model to ensure High Impact Learning that Lasts. For example, it is recommended that in knowledge acquisition phases, an appropriate amount of information and adequate examples should be provided to the learners. In capacity-building phases, learners should be stimulated to learn through trial-and-error. Although the list is not meant to be complete, Table 6.2 does elaborate on suggested suitable activities to support High Impact Learning in the different learning phases. These may be used as inspiration for instructors as well as designers of learning trajectories to contribute to the development of impactful lifelong learning trajectories.

TABLE 6.2

Preparation phase	• Use authentic, real-world, work-based problems and cases. • An assessment should take the place of the pre-existing knowledge of the individual learner. • Provide self-assessment for gauging learners' strengths, weaknesses, interests and motivation. • Allow learners to set personalised learning goals and objectives. • Leverage the benefits of ICT tools regarding pre-assessment. • Discuss learners' perspectives on the urgency/work-based problems/gap. Co-create learner awareness on the intention and benefits of the learning trajectory. • Let learners demonstrate pre-knowledge to enable transfer to the rest of his or her learning path.
Knowledge acquisition phase	• Use authentic, real-world, work-based problems and cases. • Allow for learners to do self-management: to set learning goals, to self-reflect and to perform self-assessment. • Provide an appropriate amount of information to enable knowledge acquisition using a variety of examples and contexts. • Leverage the benefits of ICT tools, ensuring there is enough interaction, peer discussion and knowledge sharing. • Enable ways for instructors to provide interactive coaching to the learners. • Use (ICT-related) tools that allow for flexibility and spontaneous learning. • Use (ICT-related) tools that allow for assessment of learners' progress. • Instructor and/or ICT-related tools assess the learning trajectories and enable transfer of learning to other phases and the workplace.
Application phase	• Use authentic, real-world, work-based problems and cases. • Allow for learners to do self-management: to set learning goals, to self-reflect and to perform self-assessment. • Provide learners with sufficient practice opportunities to allow for capacity-building using a variety of examples and contexts. • Provide feedback and coaching support that is informative and corrective to the learners to enable performance improvement and help build capacity. • Stimulate learning by doing and experimentation. Leave room for trial-and-error and spontaneous learning. • If applicable, stimulate group collaboration, fostering collaboration, interaction, knowledge sharing and networking. • Provide learners with sufficient opportunities to integrate both knowledge and capabilities by stimulating, analysing, evaluating and creating knowledge by utilising various examples and contexts. • Provide constructive coaching that is developmental and process-related to enable learners to self-integrate knowledge and capabilities. • Leave room for learners to choose different problem-solving tracks and processes. • Assess learners' progress and guide them accordingly. • Enable the transfer of learning to other phases and the workplace.

Job-setting phase	• Encourage the transfer of knowledge and capabilities towards the workplace. • Enable learners to easily repeat and practise what is learned to maintain knowledge and capability application within the job setting. • Support the development of further learning goals.

As a final remark, we acknowledge that this case analysis reported here is focused on the role of educational institutions in the realisation of lifelong learning trajectories (so-called Centres of Expertise). However, the role of the other two key players (business and government) are just as important. For example, businesses may encourage lifelong learning by encouraging PDPs or by providing employees with time to develop themselves alongside their work. Without such support, individuals are unlikely to join in lifelong learning trajectories.

Similarly, individual lifelong learning initiatives need the support of the government to become successful. In our current society, the government takes a rather static attitude towards educational processes regarding individual learning. For example, the European Credit Transfer System (ECTS) is set up in such a way that one ECTS reflects approximately 24 to 30 hours spent on studying. This system is incompatible with the recognition of individual, on-demand and just-in-time learning as professionals are unlikely to spend enough time on the same topic to gain such credits. And without such credits, the learning is not recognised. By introducing a more flexible system, the government could support individual, on-demand and just-in-time lifelong learning. However, similar to future research for businesses, insights into how the government could best support lifelong learning initiatives and spread awareness are needed.

In this case analysis, we have provided some insights into how individual, on-demand and just-in-time lifelong learning may be developed in the upcoming years. It only takes a little imagination to take it a step further and think about what the future of learning may look like. How may the future look like if we look ahead to 15, 20 or even 100 years from now?

Imagine if we could produce some sort of 'knowledge-pills' that would allow us to consume knowledge that is ready to use at any time and place? It would certainly save us a lot of energy and time, normally invested in going to educational institutions and studying. Unfortunately, we are nowhere close to a learning product like this.

Nevertheless, bright people among us are working on the next best thing. For example, during the project we stumbled upon the concept of virtual reality. It can simulate highly specific experiences that would otherwise not be possible, at least not for the masses. It creates the possibility of being present in any environment at any place in time.

Let's stay in the technology sector and say you want to learn more about building robots. Imagine how expensive it would be: gathering all the parts together, trying to make new ideas work, and along the way some parts may break which you would have to replace. Using virtual reality learning, you may be present at home while you are virtually able to work, learn and play around with the concept of building robots. Imagine what we could all build together, if we were all able to learn any time, any place and any subject that would otherwise not be possible?

The future of learning lies ahead of us and we are slowly moving towards great new things. First classroom learning, then online learning and who knows what will come next. The only thing that we can be sure of is that the concept of learning, the tools and the trajectories will develop themselves in order to fit with the current needs of the people. And who knows – maybe one day we will be able to download all the knowledge we wish onto a personal chip that is implanted into our brains?

Note

1 Thanks to Jos van Erp, Selma van der Haar, Evy van Dierendonck, Agnieszka Drożdżal, Romy Hermans, Thom Lunenborg, Aniek Mölenberg and Paul Wanders for their preparatory work, data-gathering and reporting.

Bibliography

Actie Agenda Smart Industry: Dutch Industry Fit for the Future (2014). Retrieved from www.smartindustry.nl/publicaties

Allen, J., & De Grip, A. (2007). *Skill obsolescence, lifelong learning and labor market participation.* Maastricht, the Netherlands: Research Centre for Education and the Labour Market (ROA), Faculty of Economics and Business Administration, Maastricht University.

Allen, J., & De Grip, A. (2012). Does skill obsolescence increase the risk of employment loss? *Applied Economics, 44*(25), 3237–3245.

Baldwin, T. T., & Ford, J. K. (1988). Transfer of training: A review and directions for future research. *Personnel Psychology, 41*(1), 63–105.

Benigno, V., & Trentin, G. (2000). The evaluation of online courses. *Journal of Computer Assisted Learning, 16*(3), 259–270.

Biggs, J. (1999). What the student does: Teaching for enhanced learning. *Higher Education Research & Development, 18*(1), 57–75.

Bloom, B. S. (1965). *Bloom's taxonomy of educational objectives.* New York: Longman.

Bonakdarian, E., Whittaker, T., & Yang, Y. (2010). Mixing it up: More experiments in hybrid learning. *Journal of Computing Sciences in Colleges, 25*(4), 97–103.

Broad, M. L., & Newstrom, J. W. (1992). *Transfer of training: Action-packed strategies to ensure high payoff from training investments.* Reading: Addison-Wesley Publishing Co.

Broek, S, & Buiskool, G. (2012). Mapping and comparing mobilisation strategies throughout Europe: Towards making lifelong learning a reality. *Journal of Adult and Continuing Education, 18*(1), 4–26.

Cameron, J., & Pierce, W. D. (1994). Reinforcement, reward, and intrinsic motivation: A meta-analysis. *Review of Educational research, 64*(3), 363–423.

Cavus, N., Uzunboylu, H., & Ibrahim, D. (2007). Assessing the success rate of students using a learning management system together with a collaborative tool in web-based teaching of programming languages. *Journal of Educational Computing Research, 36*(3), 301–321.

Chen, P. S. D., Lambert, A. D., & Guidry, K. R. (2010). Engaging online learners: The impact of web-based learning technology on college student engagement. *Computers & Education, 54*(4), 1222–1232.

Chesbrough, H., Vanhaverbeke, W., & West, J. (Eds.) (2014). *New frontiers in open innovation.* Oxford: Oxford University Press.

Clark-Ibáñez, M., & Scott, L. (2008). Learning to teach online. *Teaching Sociology, 36*(1), 34–41.

D'Abate, C. P., Eddy, E. R., & Tannenbaum, S. I. (2003). What's in a name? A literature-based approach to understanding mentoring, coaching, and other constructs that describe developmental interactions. *Human Resource Development Review, 2*(4), 360–384.

De Grip, A., & Van Loo, J. (2002). The economics of skills obsolescence: A review. *The economics of Skills Obsolescence: Theoretical Innovations and Empirical Applications, 21,* 1–26.

Dochy, F., Berghmans, I., Koenen, A. K., & Segers, M., (2015). *Bouwstenen voor High Impact Learning* [Building blocks for High Impact Learning]. Amsterdam, the Netherlands: Boom.

Dochy, F., & Segers, M. (1999). *Innovatieve toetsvormen als gevolg van constructiegericht student georiënteerd onderwijs: op weg naar een assessmentcultuur. Meer kansen creëren in het hoger onderwijs* [Innovative modes of assessment as a consequence of student oriënted education: A way to a new assessment culture. Creating more chances in higher education]. Mechelen, Belgium: Kluwer Editorial.

Dochy, F., Gijbels, D., Segers, M. & Van den Bossche, P. (2010). *Theories of learning for the workplace: Building blocks for training and professional development programs.* London: Routledge.

Downes, S. (2014). *MOOC: The Massive Open Online Course in theory and in practice.* Retrieved from www.slideshare.net/Downes/xmooc-the-massive-open-online-course-in-theory-and-in-practice

Drucker, P. (2014). *Innovation and entrepreneurship.* London: Routledge.

Ennis, S., Goodman, R., Hodgetts, W., Hunt, J., Mansfield, R., Otto, J., & Stern, L. (2005). *Core competencies of the executive coach.* Retrieved from www.executivecoachingforum.com/

Ericsson, K. A. (2016). *Peak: Secrets from the new science of expertise.* Boston, MA: Houghton Mifflin Harcourt.

European Commission. (2016). *Demographic analysis.* Retrieved from: http://ec.europa.eu/social/main.jsp?catId=502

Gerards, R., De Grip, A., Hoon, M., Kühn-Nelen, A. C., & Poulissen, D. (2015). *Arbeidsmarktmonitor Metalektro 2014* [Labour market monitor for the metal and electrics industry sector 2014]. Maastricht, the Netherlands: ROA, Maastricht University School of Business and Economics.

Goodyear, P., Salmon, G., Spector, J. M., Steeples, C., & Tickner, S. (2001). Competences for online teaching: A special report. *Educational Technology Research and Development, 49*(1), 65–72.

Graesser, A. C., Conley, M. W., & Olney, A. (2012). Intelligent tutoring systems. *Educational Psychology Handbook, 3,* 451–473.

Grief, S. (2007). Advances in research on coaching outcomes. *International Coaching Psychology Review, 2,* 222–249.

Griffiths, K. E. (2005). Personal coaching: A model for effective learning. *Journal of Learning Design, 1*(2), 55–65.

Hirsch, B., & Ng, J. W. (2011). Education beyond the cloud: Anytime-anywhere learning in a smart campus environment. *2011 International Conference for Internet Technology and Secured Transactions (ICITST)* (pp. 718–723), Abu Dhabi, United Arab Emirates. IEEE.

Holton, E. F. (1996). The flawed four-level evaluation model. *Human Resource Development Quarterly, 7*(1), 5–21.

Holton, E. F., & Baldwin, T. T. (Eds.) (2003). Making transfer happen: An action perspective on learning transfer systems. In *Improving learning transfer in organizations* (pp. 3–15). San Francisco, CA: Jossey-Bass.

Jaspers, M., & Heijmen-Versteegen, I. (2004). *Toetswijzer competentiegericht begeleiden en beoordelen in het hoger onderwijs* [Guide for assessment of competence-oriented support and evaluation in higher education]. Eindhoven: Fontys School for Higher Vocattional Education.

Kagermann, H., Wahlster, W., & Helbig, J. (2013). *Recommendations for implementing the strategic initiative INDUSTRIE 4.0.* Retrieved from the Acatech website: www.acatech.de/fileadmin/user_upload/Baumstruktur_nach_Website/Acatech/root/de/Material_fuer_Sonderseiten/Industrie_4.0/Final_report__Industrie_4.0_accessible.pdf

Kilburg, R. R. (1996). Toward a conceptual understanding and definition of executive coaching. *Consulting Psychology Journal: Practice and Research, 48*(2), 134–144.

Kim, J. S. (2005). The effects of a constructivist teaching approach on student academic achievement, self-concept, and learning strategies. *Asia Pacific Education Review, 6*(1), 7–19.

Krathwohl, D. R. (2002). A revision of Bloom's taxonomy: An overview. *Theory into Practice, 41*(4), 212–218.

Kulik, J. A., & Fletcher, J. D. (2016). Effectiveness of Intelligent Tutoring Systems: A meta-analytic review. *Review of Educational Review, 86*(1), 42–78.

Lane, L. (2012). *Three kinds of MOOC.* Lisa's (online) teaching & history blog. Retrieved from https://lisahistoryblog.wordpress.com/2012/08/15/three-kinds-of-moocs/

Lee, E. A. (2008). Cyber physical systems: Design challenges. In *2008 11th IEEE International Symposium on Object Oriented Real-Time Distributed Computing (ISORC)* (pp. 363–369), Orlando, Florida: IEEE.

Lee, J. (2010). Design of blended training for transfer into the workplace. *British Journal Educational Technology, 41*(2), 181–198.

Liu, C., Zhong, Y., Ozercan, S., & Zhu, Q. (2013). Facilitating 3D virtual world learning environments creation by non-technical end users through template-based virtual world instantiation. *International Journal of Virtual and Personal Learning Environments (IJVPLE), 4*(1), 32–48.

Margaryan, A., Bianco, M., & Littlejohn, A. (2015). Instructional quality of massive open online courses (MOOCs). *Computers & Education, 80*, 77–83.

Merrill, M. D. (2002). First principles of instruction. *Educational Technology Research and Development, 50*(3), 43–59.

Poell, R. F. (2006). Organizing learning projects whilst improving work: Strategies of employees, managers, and HRD professionals. In J. N. Streumer (Ed.), *Work-related learning* (pp. 151–180). Dordrecht: Springer.

Renkl, A., & Atkinson, R. K. (2007). Interactive learning environments: Contemporary issues and trends. An introduction to the special issue. *Educational Psychology Review, 19*(3), 235–238.

Roco, M. C., & Bainbridge, W. S. (2013). The new world of discovery, invention, an innovation: Convergence of knowledge, technology, and society. *Journal of Nanoparticle Research, 15*(9), 1–17.

Rubens, N., Kaplan, D., & Okamoto, T. (2012). E-Learning 3.0: Anyone, anywhere, anytime, and AI. In *New horizons in web based learning* (pp. 171–180). Berlin; Heidelberg, Germany: Springer Berlin Heidelberg.

Russell, D. M., Klemmer, S., Fox, A., Latulipe, C., Duneier, M., & Losh, E. (2013). Will massive online open courses (MOOCs) change education? *CHI'13 extended abstracts on Human Factors in Computing Systems* (pp. 2395–2398). New York, NY: ACM.

Siemens, G. (2005). Connectivism: Learning as network-creation. *elearnspace.* Retrieved from www.elearnspace.org/Articles/networks.htm

Siemens, G. (2013). Massive open online courses: Innovation in education. *Open Educational Resources: Innovation, Research and Practice, 5*, 5–15.

Sierens, E. Vansteenkiste, M., Goossens, L., Soenens, B., & Dochy, F. (2009). The synergistic relationship of perceived autonomy support and structure in the prediction of self-regulated learning. *British Journal of Educational Psychology, 79*(1), 57–68.

Slavin, R. E. (1983). When does cooperative learning increase student achievement? *Psychological Bulletin, 94*(3), 429–445.

Smith, B., & Eng, M. (2013). MOOCs: A learning journey. In S. K. S. Cheung, J. Fong, W. Fong, F. L. Wang, & L. F. Kwok (Eds.), *Hybrid learning and continuing education* (pp. 244–255). Berlin: Springer Berlin Heidelberg.

Spitzer, M. (2006). Brain research and learning over the life cycle. In OECD Organisation for Economic Co-operation and Development (Ed.), *Schooling for tomorrow: Personalising education* (pp. 47–62). Paris, France: OECD/CERI.

Srebrenkoska, V., Mitrev, S., Atanasova-Pacemska, T., & Karov, I. (2014). *Lifelong learning for creativity and innovation.* Presented at the International Scientific Conference of Gabrovo, Bulgaria.

Stevens, V. (2013). What's with the MOOCs? *TESL-EJ, 16*(4), 1–14.

Thijssen, J. G., Van der Heijden, B. I., & Rocco, T. S. (2008). Toward the employability–link model: Current employment transition to future employment perspectives. *Human Resource Development Review, 7*(2), 165–183.

Van Bruggen, L., & Ritzen, M. M. J. (2010). Assessen van competentiegericht onderwijs [Assessment of competence-oriented education]. *Onderwijsvernieuwing, 14*, 17–20.

Van Erp, J. (2015). *Bedrijven, scholen en arbeidsmarkt. Een grensoverschrijdende zoektocht naar evenwicht* [Companies, school and the labour market: A boundary-crossing search for equilibrium]. Unpublished report.

Van Roosmalen, G., Berghmans, I., Brants, L., Struyven, K., & Vierendeels, R. (2010). *Studenten leren van studenten. PAL inspiratiegids* [Students learn from students. PAL (Peer Assisted Learning) inspirational guide]. Leuven, Belgium: KU Leuven.

Vandeput, L., Tambuyser, L., & De Gruyter, J. (2011). *Van e-learning naar geïntegreerd blended learning* [From e-learning to integrated blended learning]. Katholieke Universiteit Leuven. Leuven, Belgium: KU Leuven.

Wagner, E. D. (1994). In support of a functional definition of interaction. *American Journal of Distance Education, 8*(2), 6–29.

Wilson, G., & Stacey, E. (2004). Online interaction impacts on learning: Teaching the instructors to teach online. *Australasian Journal of Educational Technology, 20*(1), 33–48.

Zimmerman, B. J., Bonner, S., & Kovach, R. (1996). *Developing self-regulated learners: Beyond achievement to self-efficacy.* Washington, DC: American Psychological Association.

BIBLIOGRAPHY

Ackland, R. (1991). A review of the peer coaching literature. *Journal of Staff Development,* *12*(1), 22–27.

Baars, M.,Van Gog,T., de Bruin,A., & Paas, F. (2017). Effects of problem solving after worked example study on secondary school children's monitoring accuracy. *Educational Psychology,* *37*(7), 810–834.

Baas, D. (2017). *Assessment for Learning: More than a tool.* Maastricht: Datawyse/Universitaire Pers Maastricht.

Baert, H. (2017). Informal learning at work: What do we know more and understand better? In G. Messmann, M. Segers & F. Dochy (Eds.), *Informal learning at work: Triggers, antecedents and consequences.* London: Routledge.

Barendsen, M., & Dochy, F. (2017). *Team coaching: Exploring the different team coaching behaviours and the importance of team coaching for organisations.* Unpublished research report.

Beausaert, S. (2011). *The use of Personal Development Plans in the workplace: Effects, purposes and supporting conditions.* Maastricht: Datawyse/Universitaire Pers Maastricht.

Bell, B. S., & Kozlowski, S.W. (2008).Active learning: Effects of core training design elements on self-regulatory processes, learning, and adaptability. *Journal of Applied Psychology, 93*(2), 296–316.

Bernard, R., Borokhovski, E., Schmid, R. F.,Tamim, R., & Abrami, P. (2014).A meta-analysis of blended learning and technology use in higher education: From the general to the applied. *Journal of Computing in Higher Education, 26*(1), 87–122.

Besieux,T. (2017).Why I hate feedback: Anchoring effective feedback within organizations. *Business Horizons, 60*(4), 435–439.

Birenbaum, M., & Dochy, F. (Eds.) (1996). *Alternatives in assessment of achievements, learning processes and prior knowledge. Evaluation in education and human services.* Boston, MA: Kluwer Academic Publishers.

Black, P., & Wiliam, D. (1998). Assessment and classroom learning. *Assessment in Education: Principles, Policy & Practice, 5*(1), 7–74.

Boekaerts, M., & Corno, L. (2005). Self-regulation in the classroom: A perspective on assessment and intervention. *Applied Psychology, 54*(2), 199–231.

Boon, A., Raes, E., Kyndt, E., & Dochy, F. (2013).Team learning beliefs and behaviours in response teams. *European Journal of Training and Development, 37*(4), 357–379.

Boon, A., Vangrieken, K., & Dochy, F. (2016). Team creativity versus team learning: Transcending conceptual boundaries for future framework building. *Human Resource Development International, 19*(1), 67–90.

Bowen, C. W. (2000). A quantitative literature review of cooperativie learning effects on high school and college chemistry achievement. *Journal of Chemical Education, 77*(1), 116–119.

Braxton, J. M., Milem, J. F., & Sullivan, A. S. (2000). The influence of active learning on the college student departure process: Toward a revision of Tinto's theory. *The Journal of Higher Education, 71*(5), 569–590.

Bruffee, K. A. (1995). Sharing our toys: Cooperative learning versus collaborative learning. *Change: The Magazine of Higher Learning, 27*(1), 12–18.

Bruner, J. S. (1996). *The culture of education.* Cambridge, MA: Harvard University Press.

Burke, L. A., & Hutchins, H. M. (2007). A study of best practices in training transfer and proposed model of transfer. *Human Resource Development Quarterly, 19*(2), 107–128.

Butler, D. L., & Winne, P. H. (1995). Feedback and self-regulated learning: A theoretical synthesis. *Review of Educational Research, 65*(3), 245–281.

Carolus, L., & Dochy, F. (2017). *Blended learning in organisations: A qualitative mixed method study about blended learning in corporate training settings.* Leuven: KU Leuven, unpublished report.

Cascio, W. F. (2015). Strategic HRM: Too important for an insular approach. *Human Resource Management, 54*(3), 423–426.

Cerasoli, C. P., Nicklin, J. M., & Ford, M. T. (2014). Intrinsic motivation and extrinsic incentives jointly predict performance: A 40-year meta-analysis. *Psychological Bulletin, 140*(4), 980–1008.

CIPD (2016). CIPD Learning and Development Show 2016: Employee-led, integrated learning is the new normal. Retrieved from www.cipd.co.uk/about/media/press/110516-ld-show

Colardyn, D., & Bjornavold, J. (2004). Validation of formal, non-formal and informal learning: Policy and practices in EU member states. *European Journal of Education, 39*(1), 69–89.

Cusumano, M. A. (2014). MOOCs revisited, with some policy suggestions. *Communications of the ACM, 57*(4), 24–26.

Csikszentmihalyi, M., & Beattie, O. (1979). Life themes: A theoretical and empirical exploration of their origins and effects. *Journal of Humanistic Psychology, 19*(1), 45–63.

Davies, A., Fidler, D., & Gorbis, M. (2011). *Future work skills 2020.* Institute for the Future for University of Phoenix Research Institute.

Day, J. A. (2008). *Investigating learning with web lectures* (Unpublished doctoral dissertation). Georgia Institute of Technology. Retrieved from http://smartech.gatech.edu/handle/1853/22627

Day, J. A., & Foley, J. D. (2006). Evaluating a web lecture intervention in a human–computer interaction course. *IEEE Transactions on Education, 49*(4), 420–431.

De Corte, E. (1995). Learning theory and instructional science. In P. Reiman & H. Spada (Eds.), *Learning in humans and machines: Towards an interdisciplinary learning science* (pp. 97–108). Oxford: Elsevier Science.

De Corte, E. (1996). Active learning within powerful learning environment. *Impuls, 26*(4), 145–156.

Dewey, J. (1938). *Experience and education.* New York, NY: Macmillan.

Deci, E. L., Koestner, R., & Ryan, R. M. (1999). A meta-analytic review of experiments examining the effects of extrinsic rewards on intrinsic motivation. *Psychological Bulletin, 125*(6), 627–668.

Decuyper, S., Dochy, F., & Van den Bossche, P. (2010). Grasping the dynamic complexity of team learning: An integrative model for effective team learning in organisations. *Educational Research Review, 5*(2), 111–133.

Deslauriers, L., Schelew, E., & Wieman, C. (2011). Improved learning in a large-enrollment physics class. *Science, 332*(6031), 862–864.

Dochy, F. (1992). *Assessment of prior knowledge as a determinant for future learning: The use of prior knowledge state tests and knowledge profiles.* London: Jessica Kingsley Publishers.

Dochy, F., & James, M. (2017). Assessment as Learning: personal communication.

Dochy, F., Segers, M., Van den Bossche, P., & Gijbels, D. (2003). Effects of problem-based learning: A meta-analysis. *Learning and Instruction, 13*(5), 533–568.

Dochy, F., Engeström, Y., Sannino, A., & Van Meeuwen, N. (2011). Inter-organisational expansive learning at work. In F. Dochy, D. Gijbels, M. Segers, & P. Van den Bossche (Eds.), *Theories of learning for the workplace: Building blocks for training and professional development programs* (pp. 125–147). London: Routledge.

Dochy, F., Gijbels, D., Raes, E., & Kyndt, E. (2014). Team learning in education and professional organisations. In S. Billett, C. Harteis, & H. Gruber (Eds.), *International handbook of research in professional and practice-based learning* (pp. 987–1020). Dordrecht, the Netherlands: Springer Netherlands.

Dochy, F., Berghmans, I., Koenen, A., & Segers, M. (2015). *Bouwstenen voor High Impact Learning. Het leren van de toekomst in onderwijs en organisaties* [Building blocks for high impact learning: Future learning in education and in organisations]. Amsterdam, the Netherlands: Boom Uitgevers.

Dziuban, C. D., Hartman, J., Juge, F., Moskal, P. D., & Sorg, S. (2005). Blended learning: Online learning enters the mainstream. In C. J. Bonk & C. R. Graham (Eds.), *Handbook of blended learning environment: Global perspectives, local designs* (pp. 195–208). San Francisco, CA: Pfeiffer Publishing.

Edmondson, A. (1999). Psychological safety and learning behavior in work teams. *Administrative Science Quarterly, 44*(2), 350–383.

Elvira, Q., Imants, J., Dankbaar, B., & Segers, M. (2016). Designing education for professional expertise development. *Scandinavian Journal of Educational Research, 23*, 1–18.

Elvira, Q., Imants, J., DeMayer, S., & Segers, M. (2016). The quality of high school students' problem solving from an expertise development perspective. *Citizenship, Social and Economics Education, 14*(3), 172–192.

Emonds, A., Dochy, F., & Segers, M. (2017). A climate for learning – six dimensions to target when changing your corporate learning climate. Retrieved from www.crossknowledge.com/en-gb/webinar-uk

Eraut, M. (2004). Informal learning in the workplace. *Studies in Continuing Education, 26*(2), 247–273.

Ericsson, K. A. (2016). *Peak: Secrets from the new science of expertise.* Boston, MA: Houghton Mifflin Harcourt.

Eteläpelto, A., Vähäsantanen, K., Hökkä, P., & Paloniemi, S. (2013). What is agency? Conceptualizing professional agency at work. *Educational Research Review, 10*, 45–65.

Fox, D. (2017). Personal communication.

Freeman, S., Eddy, S. L., McDonough, M., Smith, M. K., Okoroafor, N., Jordt, H., & Wenderoth, M. P. (2014). Active learning increases student performance in science, engineering, and mathematics. *Proceedings of the National Academy of Sciences, 111*(23), 8410–8415.

Friedman, M. (2016). *A theory of the consumption function.* San Francisco, CA: Pickle Partners Publishing.

Froehlich, D. E., Beausaert, S., & Segers, M. (2017). Development and validation of a scale measuring approaches to work-related informal learning. *International Journal of Training and Development, 21*(2), 130–144.

Froehlich, D., Beausaert, S., Segers, M., & Gerken, M. (2014). Learning to stay employable. *Career Development International, 19*(5), 508–525.

Gabelica, C., Van den Bossche, P., Segers, M., & Gijselaers, W. (2012). Feedback, a powerful lever in teams: A review. *Educational Research Review, 7*(2), 123–144.

Gabelica, C., Van den Bossche, P., De Maeyer, S., Segers, M., & Gijselaers, W. (2014). The effect of team feedback and guided reflexivity on team performance change. *Learning and Instruction, 34*, 86–96.

Gao, X., & Zhang, L. J. (2011). Joining forces for synergy: Agency and metacognition as interrelated theoretical perspectives on learner autonomy. In G. Murray, Z. Gao & T. Lam (Eds.), *Identity, motivation and autonomy in language learning* (pp. 25–41). Bristol: Multilingual Matters.

Garrison, R., & Kanuka, H. (2004). Blended learning: Uncovering its transformative potential in higher education. *The Internet and Higher Education, 7*, 95–105.

Gerken, M., Beausaert, S., & Segers, M. (2016). Working on professional development of faculty staff in higher education: Investigating the relationship between social informal learning activities and employability. *Human Resource Development International, 19*(2), 135–151.

Govaerts, N. (2017). *Transfer of training: Understanding the multidimensional role of supervisor support* (Doctoral dissertation). Leuven: KU Leuven.

Grabinger, S., Dunlap, J., & Duffield, J. (1997). Rich environments for active learning in action: Problem-based learning. *Association for Learning Technology Journal, 5*(2), 5–17.

Graham, C. R. (2006). Blended learning systems: Definition, current trends and future directions. In C. J. Bonk & C. R. Graham (Eds.), *Handbook of blended learning: Global perspectives, local designs*. San Francisco, CA: Pfeiffer. Retrieved from www.click4it.org/images/a/a8/Graham.pdf

Grosemans, I., & Kyndt, E. (2015). *Transition from higher education to work: State of the art*. Paper presented at the Biennial EARLI conference, Limassol, Cyprus.

Hackman, J. R., & Wageman, R. (2005). A theory of team coaching. *Academy of Management Review, 30*(2), 269–287.

Harlen, W., & James, M. (1997). Assessment and learning: Differences and relationships between formative and summative assessment. *Assessment in Education: Principles, Policy & Practice, 4*(3), 365–379.

Helle, L., Tynjälä, P., & Olkinuora, E. (2006). Project-based learning in post-secondary education – theory, practice and rubber sling shots. *Higher Education, 51*(2), 287–314.

Heylighen, A., & Neuckermans, H. (2000). DYNAMO: Dynamic architectural memory online. *Educational Technology and Society, 3*(2), 86–95.

Hmelo-Silver, C. E. (2004). Problem-based learning: What and how do students learn? *Educational Psychology Review, 16*(3), 235–266.

Howlett, D., Vincent, T., Watson, G., Owens, E., Webb, R., Gainsborough, N., & Vincent, R. (2011). Blending online techniques with traditional face to face teaching methods to deliver final year undergraduate radiology learning content. *European Journal of Radiology, 78*, 334–341.

Iverson, K. M., Colky, D. L., & Cyboran, V. L. (2005). E-learning takes the lead: An empirical investigation of learner differences in online and classroom delivery. *Performance Improvement Quarterly, 18*(4), 5–18.

James, M. (2006) Assessment, teaching and theories of learning. In J. Gardner (Ed.), *Assessment and learning* (pp. 47–60). London: Sage.

James, M. (2011). Assessment for learning: Research and policy in the (dis)United Kingdom. In R. Berry & R. Adamson (Eds.), *Assessment reform in education* (15–32). New York, NY: Springer.

James, M. (2012). Assessment in harmony with our understanding of learning: Problems and possibilities. In J. Gardner (Ed.), *Assessment and learning* (2nd ed., pp. 187–205). London: Sage.

Johnson, D. W., & Johnson, R. T. (2009). An educational psychology success story: Social interdependence theory and cooperative learning. *Educational Researcher, 38*(5), 365–379.

Johnson, D., Johnson, R. T., & Tjosvold, D. (2000). Constructive controversy: The value of intellectual opposition. In M. Deutsch & P. T. Coleman (Eds.), *The handbook of conflict resolution: Theory and practice* (pp. 65–85). San Francisco, CA: Jossey-Bass Publishers.

Johnson, D. W., Johnson, R. T., & Stanne, M. B. (2000). *Cooperative learning methods: A meta-analysis.* Minneapolis, MN: University of Minnesota Press.

Jones, G., & Sallis, E. (2013). *Knowledge management in education: Enhancing learning & education.* London: Routledge.

Joyce, B., & Showers, B. (1980). Improving inservice training: The messages of research. *Educational Leadership, 37*(5), 379–385.

Kingston, N., & Nash, B. (2011). Formative assessment: A meta-analysis and a call for research. *Educational Measurement: Issues and Practice, 30*(4), 28–37.

Kluger, A. N., & DeNisi, A. (1996). The effects of feedback interventions on performance: A historical review, a meta-analysis, and a preliminary feedback intervention theory. *Psychological Bulletin, 119*(2), 254–284.

Koenen, A., Dochy, F., & Berghmans, I. (2015). A phenomenographic analysis of the implementation of competence-based education in higher education. *Teaching and Teacher Education, 50,* 1–12.

Koh, G. C. H., Khoo, H. E., Wong, M. L., & Koh, D. (2008). The effects of problem-based learning during medical school on physician competency: A systematic review. *Canadian Medical Association Journal, 178*(1), 34–41.

Kolb, D. A. (1984). *Experiential learning.* Englewood Cliffs, NJ: Prentice-Hall.

Konradt, U., Otte, K. P., Schippers, M. C., & Steenfatt, C. (2016). Reflexivity in teams: A review and new perspectives. *The Journal of Psychology, 150*(2), 153–174.

Kyndt, E., & Baert, H. (2013). Antecedents of employees' involvement in work-related learning: A systematic review. *Review of Educational Research, 83*(2), 273–313.

Kyndt, E., Govaerts, N., Smet, K., & Dochy, F. (2017). Factors influencing informal workplace learning: A theoretical study. In G. Messmann, M. Segers & F. Dochy (Eds.), *Informal learning at work: Triggers, antecedents and consequences.* London: Routledge.

Kyndt, E., Raes, E., Lismont, B., Timmers, F., Cascallar, E., & Dochy, F. (2013). A meta-analysis of the effects of face-to-face cooperative learning: Do recent studies falsify or verify earlier findings? *Educational Research Review, 10,* 133–149.

Lazonder, A., & Harmsen, R. (2016). Meta-analysis of inquiry-based learning: Effects of guidance. *Review of Educational Research, 86*(3), 681–718.

Lee, E. A. (2008). Cyber physical systems: Design challenges. In *2008 11th IEEE International Symposium on Object Oriented Real-Time Distributed Computing (ISORC)* (pp. 363–369), Orlando, FL: IEEE.

Lim, D. H., & Morris, M. L. (2009). Learner and instructional factors influencing learning outcomes within a blended learning environment. *Educational Technology & Society, 12*(4), 282–293.

Lim, D. H., Morris, M. L., & Kupritz, V. W. (2007). Online vs. blended learning: Differences in instructional outcomes and learner satisfaction. *Journal of Asynchronous Learning Networks, 11*(2), 27–42.

Liu, Q., Peng, W., Zhang, F., Hu, R., Li, Y., & Yan, W. (2016). The effectiveness of blended learning in health professions: Systematic review and meta-analysis. *Journal of Medical Internet Research, 18*(1).

Lu, H. L. (2010). Research on peer coaching in preservice teacher education: A review of literature. *Teaching and Teacher Education, 26*(4), 748–753.

Manuti, A., Pastore, S., Scardigno, A. F., Giancaspro, M. L., & Morciano, D. (2015). Formal and informal learning in the workplace: A research review. *International Journal of Training and Development, 19*(1), 1–17.

Marsick, V. J., & Watkins, K. E. (2001). Informal and incidental learning. *New Directions for Adult and Continuing Education, 89*, 25–34.

Martin, J. (2004). Self-regulated learning, social cognitive theory, and agency. *Educational Psychologist, 39*(2), 135–145.

Marton, F. (1999). Personal communication.

Mathieu, J., Maynard, M. T., Rapp, T., & Gilson, L. (2008). Team effectiveness 1997–2007: A review of recent advancements and a glimpse into the future. *Journal of Management, 34*(3), 410–476.

McKeachie, W. J., Pintrich, P., Lin, Y., & Smith, D. (1986). *Teaching and learning in the college classroom: A review of the research literature (and November 1987 supplement)*. Ann Arbor, MI: National Center for Research to Improve Post-Secondary Teaching and Learning.

Means, B., Toyama, Y., Murphy, R., Bakia, M., & Jones, K. (2009). *Evaluation of evidence-based practices in online learning: A meta-analysis and review of online learning studies*. Washington, DC: US Department of Education.

Mercer, S. (2013). Working with language learner histories from three perspectives: Teachers, learners and researchers. *Studies in Second Language Learning and Teaching, 3*(2), 161–185.

Michael, J. (2006). Where's the evidence that active learning works? *Advances in Physiology Education, 30*(4), 159–167.

Montrieux, M., Vangestel, S., Raes, A., Matthys, P., & Schellens, S. (2014). Blending face-to-face higher education with web-based lectures: Comparing different didactical intended purposes. *Educational Technology & Society, 18*(1), 170–182.

Morin, L., & Renaud, S. (2004). Participation in corporate university training: Its effect on individual job performance. *Canadian Journal of Administrative Sciences/Revue Canadienne des Sciences de l'Administration, 21*(4), 295–306.

Mulder, R. H. (2013). Exploring feedback incidents, their characteristics and the informal learning activities that emanate from them. *European Journal of Training and Development, 37*(1), 49–71.

Mulryan-Kyne, C. (2010). Teaching large classes at college and university level: Challenges and opportunities. *Teaching in Higher Education, 15*(2), 175–185.

Noe, R. A., Tews, M. J., & Marand, A. D. (2013). Individual differences and informal learning in the workplace. *Journal of Vocational Behavior, 83*(3), 327–335.

Owston, R., York, D., & Murtha, S. (2013). Student perceptions and achievement in a university blended learning strategic initiative. *The Internet and Higher Education, 18*, 38–46.

Panda, A., Karve, S., & Mohapatra, D. (2014). Aligning learning & development strategy with business: Strategy to operations. *South Asian Journal of Human Resources Management, 1*(2), 267–281.

Panitz, E. (1996). Strategic types and growth strategies used by public accounting firms. *Journal of Professional Services Marketing, 13*(1), 135–143.

Paris, S. G., & Paris, A. H. (2001). Classroom applications of research on self-regulated learning. *Educational Psychologist, 36*(2), 89–101.

Parker, P., Hall, D.T., & Kram, K. E. (2008). Peer coaching: A relational process for accelerating career learning. *Academy of Management Learning & Education, 7*(4), 487–503.

Pascarella, E. T., & Terenzini, P. T. (1991). *How colleges affect students*. San Francisco, CA: Jossey-Bass.

Pat-El, R. (2012). *Lost in translation: Congruency of teacher and student perceptions of assessment as a predictor of intrinsic motivation in ethnodiverse classrooms*. Leiden: Leiden University Press.

Pintrich, P. R. (1999). The role of motivation in promoting and sustaining self-regulated learning. *International Journal of Educational Research, 31*(6), 459–470.

Poikela, E., & Poikela, S. (1997). Conceptions of learning and knowledge-impacts on the implementation of problem-based learning. *Zeitschrift fur Hochschuldidactik, 1,* 8–21.

Prince, M. (2004). Does active learning work? A review of the research. *Journal of Engineering Education, 93*(3), 223–231.

Revans, R. W. (1982). *The origins and growth of action learning.* Bromley: Chartwell-Bratt.

Roehl, A., Reddy, S. L., & Shannon, G. J. (2013). The flipped classroom: An opportunity to engage millennial students through active learning. *Journal of Family and Consumer Sciences, 105*(2), 44–49.

Rosseel, P. (2017). Personal communication.

Savery, J. R., & Duffy, T. M. (1995). Problem based learning: An instructional model and its constructivist framework. *Educational Technology, 35*(5), 31–38.

Schön, D. A. (1983). *The reflective practitioner; how professionals think in action.* New York, NY: Basic Books.

Schwellnus, H., & Carnahan, H. (2014). Peer-coaching with health care professionals: What is the current status of the literature and what are the key components necessary in peer-coaching? A scoping review. *Medical Teacher, 36*(1), 38–46.

Seaton, D. T., Bergner, Y., Chuang, I., Mitros, P., & Pritchard, D. E. (2014). Who does what in a massive open online course? *Communications of the ACM, 57*(4), 58–65.

Segers, M., & Dochy, F. (1999). *Een nieuw onderwijsmodel voor het hoger onderwijs in theorie en praktijk* [A new educational model for higher education in theory and practice]. Diegem, Belgium: Kluwer.

Segers, M., Dochy, F., & Cascallar, E. (2003). The era of assessment engineering: Changing perspectives on teaching and learning and the role of new modes of assessment. In M. Segers, F. Dochy, & E. Cascallar (Eds.), *Optimising new modes of assessment: In search of qualities and standards* (pp. 1–12). Dordrecht: Kluwer.

Senge, P. (1990). *The fifth discipline: The art and science of the learning organization.* New York, NY: Currency Doubleday.

Sierens, E., Vansteenkiste, M., Goossens, L., Soenens, B., & Dochy, F. (2007). The synergistic relationship of perceived autonomy support and structure in the prediction of self-regulated learning. *British Journal of Educational Psychology, 79*(1), 57–68.

Sitzmann, T., Kraiger, K., Stewart, D., & Wisher, R. (2006). The comparative effectiveness of web-based and classroom instruction: A meta-analysis. *Personnel Psychology, 59*(3), 623–664.

Sitzmann, T., & Ely, K. (2011). A meta-analysis of self-regulated learning in work-related training and educational attainment: What we know and where we need to go. *Psychological Bulletin, 137*(3), 421–422.

Soderquist, K., Papalexandris, A., Ioannou, G., & Prastacos, G. (2010). From task-based to competency-based: A typology and process supporting a critical HRM transition. *Personnel Review, 39*(3), 325–346.

Stevens, R. J., Slavin, R. E., & Farnish, A. M. (1991). The effects of cooperative learning and direct instruction in reading comprehension strategies on main idea identification. *Journal of Educational Psychology, 83*(1), 8–16.

Svensson, L., Ellström, P. E., & Åberg, C. (2004). Integrating formal and informal learning at work. *Journal of Workplace Learning, 16*(8), 479–491.

Taradi, S. K., Taradi, M., Radic, K., & Pokrajac, N. (2005). Blending problem-based learning with web technology positively impacts student learning outcomes in acid-base physiology. *Advances in Physiology Education, 29*(1), 35–39.

Thai, T., De Wever, B., & Valcke, M. (2015, October). Impact of different blends of learning on students performance in higher education. In *European Conference on e-Learning* (p. 744). London: Academic Conferences International Limited.

Topping, K. (2005). Trends in peer learning. *Educational Psychology, 25*(6), 631–645.

Truss, C., & Gratton, L. (1994). Strategic human resource management: A conceptual approach. *International Journal of Human Resource Management, 5*(3), 663–686.

Tynjälä, P. (2008). Perspectives into learning at the workplace. *Educational Research Review, 3*(2), 130–154.

Van den Bossche, P., Gijselaers, W. H., Segers, M., & Kirschner, P. A. (2006). Social and cognitive factors driving teamwork in collaborative learning environments: Team learning beliefs and behaviours. *Small Group Research, 37*(5), 490–521.

Van der Haar, S., Li, J., Segers, M., Jehn, K. A., & Van den Bossche, P. (2015). Evolving team cognition: The impact of team situation models on team effectiveness. *European Journal of Work and Organizational Psychology, 24*(4), 596–610.

Van der Heijde, C. M., & Van der Heijden, B. I. J. M. (2006). A competence-based and multidimensional operationalization and measurement of employability. *Human Resource Management, 45*(3), 449–476.

Van Dinther, M., Dochy, F., & Segers, M. (2011). Factors affecting students' self-efficacy in higher education. *Educational Research Review, 6*, 95–108.

Van Lier, L. (2008). Agency in the classroom. In J. P. Lantolf & M. E. Poehner (Eds.), *Sociocultural theory and the teaching of second languages* (pp. 163–186). London: Equinox.

Vaughan, N. (2007). Perspectives on blended learning in higher education. *International Journal on E-Learning, 6*(1), 81–94.

Veestraeten, M., Kyndt, E., & Dochy, F. (2014). Investigating team learning in a military context. *Vocations and Learning, 7*(1), 75–100.

Walker, A., & Leary, H. (2009). A problem based learning meta analysis: Differences across problem types, implementation types, disciplines, and assessment levels. *Interdisciplinary Journal of Problem-based Learning, 3*(1), 12–43.

Watkins, K. E., & Marsick, V. J. (1992). Towards a theory of informal and incidental learning in organizations. *International Journal of Lifelong Education, 11*(4), 287–300.

Wieman, C., & Gilbert, S. (2015). Taking a scientific approach to science education, Part II – Changing teaching: Challenges remain before universities more widely adopt research-based approaches, despite their many benefits over lecture-based teaching. *Microbe, 10*(5), 203–207.

Wieman, C., Perkins, K. &, Gilbert, S. (2010). Transforming science education at large research universities: A case study in progress. *Change: The Magazine of Higher Learning, 42*(2), 7–14.

Wiliam, D. (2011). What is assessment for learning? *Studies in Educational Evaluation, 37*(1), 3–14.

Zhao, G., Huang, R., & Lu, Z. (2005). Theory and methodology of knowledge visualization. *Open Education Research, 11*(1), 23–27.

INDEX